Hispanic Ministry in North America

Hispanic Ministry in North America

ALEX D. MONTOYA

Ministry Resources Library

Zondervan Publishing House • Grand Rapids, MI

HISPANIC MINISTRY IN NORTH AMERICA
Copyright © 1987 by Alex D. Montoya

MINISTRY RESOURCES LIBRARY
is an imprint of Zondervan Publishing House,
1415 Lake Drive, S.E., Grand Rapids, Michigan 49506.

Library of Congress Cataloging in Publication Data

Montoya, Alex D.
  Hispanic ministry in North America.

  Bibliography: p.
  1. Church work with Hispanic Americans. 2. Missions to
Hispanic Americans. I. Title.
BV4468.2.H57M66   1987   259'.08968073   87-13996
ISBN 0-310-37741-2

Edited by Joseph Comanda
Designed by Ann Cherryman

Printed in the United States of America

87 88 89 90 91 92 / EP / 10 9 8 7 6 5 4 3 2 1

CONTENTS

Preface   7

1. The Hispanic Community   9

2. The Hispanic Pastor   23

3. Effective Evangelism   37

4. Indigenous Principles at Work   53

5. Hispanics in an Anglo Church   67

6. Organization and Administration   79

7. Hispanic Men and Women   95

8. Preaching to Hispanics   109

9. Hispanic Morality   121

10. Worship and Music   135

11. Conclusion   145

Select Bibliography   155

PREFACE

A number of years ago, a veteran missionary returning to the United States made an observation that startled me. He said in effect, "Alex, I've been in Latin America for more than twenty years. But now that I'm here, I've noticed that the church in America has virtually ignored the Hispanics who live here. Here is the mission field!"

This man voiced what I have felt for many years. The twenty-million-plus Hispanics in America *have* been ignored. That is the reason why my wife and I have committed ourselves to ministry among these Hispanics.

A new wind is blowing. The American church is awakening, sensing a burden and an urgency for the spiritual needs of this segment of our population. The pages that follow grew out of questions, notes, and lectures that I was asked to deliver on numerous occasions to both Anglo and Hispanic brothers who have a burden for these people. A week at the Central America Mission headquarters, where I addressed missionaries laboring in the United States, convinced me that I should pursue publication of this material.

My heart and soul are committed to ministry among the Hispanics. If this book encourages and assists others in the same commitment, the efforts put into it will be greatly rewarded. I wrote it to help others. Take what you can use, discard the rest, and leave the chaff and imperfections at my doorstep. I do not claim originality. My motto has been, "Use it; if it works, keep on using it!" So I say to you, if you can use this information, use it!

Many people are perhaps the real authors of this book, without whose love and labor it would never have been written or published. First and foremost, my beloved wife, Favy, who provides the inspiration for all that I do. Then there are the dear people of First Fundamental Bible Church of Monterey Park, California, who taught me how to pastor and allowed me to experiment on them. The book is really written about them—their successes and their failures. My thanks also to Joanne Kajiyama, who typed the manuscript in between her duties as a schoolteacher; to my church secretarial staff for their support; to Jim Paul of CAM International, who inspired the text; to Dr. Ralph Winter, who encouraged publication; and finally to the editorial staff of Zondervan Publishing House, who saw worth in this humble work and have labored so cordially with me to make this publication a delightful experience. To God be the glory.

1

The Hispanic Community

Worthy art Thou to take the book, and to break its seals;
for Thou wast slain, and didst purchase for God with
Thy blood men from every tribe and tongue and people
and nation *(Revelation 5:9)*.

In 1970 I found myself driving through the heart of the
Hispanic community, an unincorporated portion of the vast
metropolis of Los Angeles known only as East Los Angeles.
It seemed like a foreign country to me. It felt strange to see
so many brown-faced, dark-haired people. The language,
though English, had an unfamiliar sound. It appeared to be a
community invaded by a nonindigenous people now well-
entrenched in their new land. The homes were humble yet
neat, small but full of life. Still, I wondered why I should
feel so out of place here. After all, my name is Alex Montoya.
I am an Hispanic—as Hispanic as they come.

My father's parents came from Mexico during World War I.
His father was a tall Mexican with obviously Spanish blood,
and his mother a short, stocky woman of Indian descent. My
father married a Californian of Mexican descent, so that
made me as Hispanic as can be. But something had happened to me which I have found happens to many of our
Hispanics. I had become Anglicized and had lost touch with
my people.

In my senior year of high school I felt the call to the gospel
ministry. The next four years were spent in ministerial

preparation in a Bible college where 99 percent of the students were Anglo and where everything was taught through Anglo-American lenses. Hence, I slowly became accustomed to the Anglo way of life and lost my feelings for the Hispanic community. So great was the effect upon my life that I almost lost the call to minister the gospel to my own people, the one reason for which I had left all and gone to school in the first place.

Acculturated, they call it. Now it was my turn to become acculturated again—back into a culture I had grown up in, which was clearly evident in my looks, language, and life. Now that reversal was to take place as the Lord moved me from the white suburbs to the *barrios* of the Hispanic communities. There I would find the most thrilling challenge and most fulfilling part of my life. Yet I had to learn many things about this community before I could have an effective ministry.

The Hispanic community is not one single unit but a mixture of a variety of peoples and customs. We need to understand their origins if we are to learn how to reach these masses with the gospel. The sixties brought a great emphasis on nationalistic distinctiveness within the Hispanic community. This emphasis gave rise to numerous groups endeavoring to accentuate the cultural and even political issues peculiar to them. One example of this is the Chicano movement among Mexican-Americans that gave national pride to those Hispanics in America who came from Mexico.

Anyone who wishes to minister among Hispanics in America must realize that they are not all alike, that they are, in fact, quite a diverse group. As I write, a certain young minister is having great success in reaching Hispanics. In less than one year the church has grown to almost one hundred people, but among *Salvadorans*, Hispanics from El Salvador. In another part of town, a church is composed mostly of Cubans. Not too far from us is a Cuban-American pastor working among Mexican-Americans, and he can't seem to make the church go. Part of the problem lies in his nationality. If you know Cubans and the speed with which they speak, you will understand why the Mexican-Americans are not drawn to this ministry. The Hispanic community, then, is a mixture of all these nationalities, forming a kaleidoscope of peoples. They may seem to be all the same to the untrained eye, but in reality they are as diverse a mixture as the early European immigrants to America.

I would like to present a number of peculiarities of the Hispanic community in North America. Some peculiarities are inherent to the people and thus are found throughout Latin America. I shall merely draw broad strokes to give you a general feeling toward these people. Of course, there are always exceptions, and all these characteristics may not be present in every individual or community. Much depends on the person's background and the amount of contact with the Anglo culture.

LANGUAGE

Language is the prime medium of communication. It is the greatest barrier to the spread of the gospel. As long as we understand others and are somewhat assured they can understand us, we sense a certain confidence in sharing our ideas and even ourselves. Remove the means of communication and despair sets in. Anglo-American Christianity's inability to speak the language of its southern neighbors has been a barrier to reaching Hispanics with the gospel.

The traditional American attitude has been, "This is America. We speak English here. If these people want to live here, let them learn our language." Perhaps secular people are justified in thinking that way, but when it comes to the salvation of millions of souls, we should have a more self-sacrificing attitude like Paul's (1 Corinthians 9:22).

Hispanics, we might naturally expect, all speak Spanish. Wrong! Though many Hispanics consider Spanish their mother tongue, millions of them only know smatterings of

Spanish, not even enough to make them at ease in Mexico. Only those Hispanics born and reared in Latin America are highly proficient in Spanish. Many of these come to America and never bother to learn another language. They somehow manage to survive in a country without knowing the language. My dear grandmother spent more than forty years in America without ever learning English. (Once she was watching a television commercial which said something like "Put a Dodge in your garage, honey!" She asked my father what it meant, to which he replied, "He said to put a *mariachi* in your garage." She never did get it.)

A second group of Hispanics learns to speak both English and Spanish. Through school, work, associations, and sheer determination, they pick up a working knowledge of English. You can usually tell they are primarily Spanish-speaking by their strong accents and the difficulty they have pronouncing certain English letters. *Chair* becomes *shair* and *stop* is *estop*. Yet these people know the importance of learning the national language. A young man who recently immigrated with his grade-school children greeted me with "How are you!" This startled me since I knew he was purely Spanish-speaking. When I asked him about his new vocabulary, he wisely said, "My children are in American schools and I must learn the language so I can stay up with them." He will find his efforts greatly rewarded.

This man's children are typical of a third class of Hispanics, those raised in a Spanish-speaking environment at home but in an English-speaking world outside the home. They quickly adopt English as the lingua franca and may even become ashamed of their Spanish. We had two little boys in our Sunday school typical of this group. On one occasion they became rather boisterous and unruly. My wife, as their teacher, tried in vain to quiet them and finally addressed them in Spanish saying, "If you don't behave, I'm going to tell your mother!" One replied rather forcefully, "Don't talka to me in thata way!" That was his finest English, but showed his disdain for Spanish even at an early age.

In some homes the parents take the initiative to make their children learn English, and even demand they master it. My own father set a rule at home prohibiting Spanish at dinner. He literally forced us to learn English. Most of these individuals master two languages, and depending on their environment, may adopt one over the other.

The fourth category of Hispanics are those born to bilingual parents or parents who understand Spanish but have not mastered it enough to carry on day-to-day conversations. This class will be English-speaking with very little ability to speak in Spanish. We are presently trying to teach our children Spanish, but we can foresee that it will always be a foreign language to them. Some 90 percent of our daily conversation is English, and so it becomes the same at home. They can never master Spanish where it is spoken less than 10 percent of the time and almost never in their circle of friends. By the way, all their friends are Hispanics or have Hispanic blood.

These are the major linguistic blocks in America. They range from proficient Spanish to proficient English, with a lot of "Spanglish" in between. The matter is complex, and it is heightened by the differences in origin and types of Spanish used.

ECONOMICS

The Hispanics are primarily on the lower end of the scale economically. The vast majority are lower middle class or upper lower class. The reason for this lies in their origins. Most Hispanics have come from the most desperate and deprived group in Latin America. They leave what few belongings they have to come to a land of promise flowing with milk and honey where gold can be picked off the streets. The most desperate cases make their way across deserts, seas, and rivers and brave all kinds of dangers to flee poverty, oppression, and despair in search of a better life. In

America, they take whatever jobs are available, usually the meanest. Some even become white slaves for money-hungry sharks.

Most do not come from among the professionals or from the upper class of Latin America. In fact, they are usually illiterate and unlearned. They are not, however, lazy and irresponsible. They are highly motivated, hardworking, and extremely capable of adapting themselves to their new home. They may exist for years in a community without public notice. They don't come to cause trouble but rather to lead a quiet life free from hunger, disease, and fear. They are the poor whom Christ came to save (Luke 4:18).

The economic state of many Hispanics is changing rapidly. We find many moving into the middle and upper classes of American society, and I believe the trend will accelerate as our economy improves and social mobility continues. The Hispanic community will one day have a rich and learned section to it, and we pray a great many of them will be saved.

CULTURE

I want to share a few insights into the cultural characteristics of this community. Hispanics have a number of cultural peculiarities which ought to be understood by anyone working among them. They can either be a source of great frustration if improperly understood or a great avenue of understanding and ministry to the wise.

La familia. The family is the main unit in the Hispanic community, superseding church, political parties, or any other group. Hispanics think and act as a family unit. Such units may be large, including grandfathers or great-grandfathers. They may also be small, a father and his immediate family. Whereas Anglo families may operate on a democratic basis with a certain degree of independence between married sons and fathers, Hispanic families are more totalitarian and the influence of the elder is strong enough to affect the lives of the whole clan. In evangelizing them, this structure can be either a hindrance or a help. If we try to convert a member of the family, the family ties and pressure make it very difficult for that person to make a decision for Christ independent of the entire family. But a whole family may come to Christ when the eldest member of the family is won first. Thus there is a need to find the "kingpin" and lead him or her to Christ.

The philosophy of setting the son against the father or daughter against the mother is not the wisest. The Scriptures do indicate that such will happen (Matthew 10:35), yet we must also see the wisdom in working to win over a whole family (Acts 16:31). In one case, for instance, we were successful in winning the father and mother of a rather large family. Soon after that five children, two sons-in-law, two daughters-in-law, three sisters, two aunts, and several other close relatives were brought to salvation. All this took place in the span of two months. I have seen this repeated numerous times in our ministry among Hispanics.

Machismo. The term refers to the male cult which exists among Hispanics. It is an accepted form of male chauvinism which is much easier to observe than to explain. I plan to write a separate volume on this one trait, explaining its effects upon the Latin community and the positive way the gospel is able to change, modify, and accentuate it. But for now let me just summarize what is meant by *machismo.* Maleness is highly prized among Latins. Every young boy wants to grow up to be a real man. The question is: what is a real man? To an Hispanic, a real man is one who has his wife and children in complete subjection. His word is law, and he governs with an iron fist. A real man is strong, with no physical defects, not even the wearing of glasses. A real man can drink the hardest liquor without losing his mind. A chief sport among Hispanic men is the race to empty the most cans of beer or bottles of wine. A real man is a woman's man.

Promiscuity is seen as a quality of manliness. Hence a real man is the one who can boast of all these bravados and exploits. Just listen to the ballads of the Mexican frontier or the "discussions" at a pool hall, and you will catch a glimpse of what I mean.

The gospel opposes much of these behaviors, but they are not regarded as sins by the community. You can readily understand the change the gospel and church make upon an Hispanic male. Care must be taken not to present a weak, effeminate Christ to men who pride themselves in their maleness. To lose one's maleness is to lose life itself. More will be said on this later.

Mañana. This has discouraged many a missionary and sent him home *pronto. Mañana* is the characteristic of putting off till tomorrow what most Americans would do today—or would have done yesterday. *Mañana* is what makes an Hispanic show up to dinner with a smile at 7:30 when you expected him at 5:00. He can't see why you're so upset with him; it wasn't his fault you had the dinner cooked and served by 5:15. You see, if he had invited you to dinner, he would have had you come at 5:00 but you wouldn't have eaten until 9:00. You learn quickly to grab a snack on your way to a dinner invitation. *Mañana* is when a church service is announced for 7:00 but the people don't get there until 7:30, and the preaching doesn't start until 9:00. *Mañana* is "so what's your hurry?" For time-conscious, highly scheduled Americans, this can be frustrating!

We must understand that where they come from time is not important. A man's life is not crowded with a hundred-and-one things to do. Usually one major event per day is planned and all of life surrounds it. Add to that what we have said about the family where no one can act without the directive of the eldest, and you have a somewhat tricky and touchy situation. A simple family picnic can become a real fiasco. The day arrives, and nobody has planned for it. They hurry to buy the food. When all is ready, someone remembers that the other uncle wasn't invited, and no one dares to have a family picnic without him. So they call him, but as you can imagine he has a family of his own. Before you know it, the little morning picnic turns into a huge family affair which takes all day to organize.

Respeto. Another social characteristic of Hispanics is having high veneration or respect, *"respeto,"* for older people. Whereas American society places great value on youthfulness and genius, Hispanics place great value on age. The Spanish language has two words for *you,* one for the equal (*tu*) and another for a superior (*usted*). Parents demand the latter from their children. My father would say to me, "Don't call me *tu;* I'm not your brother."

Hence one rarely contradicts or speaks down to one's elder. Grandparents are deeply venerated. Older doctors are preferred over younger specialists. One lady refused to have a young specialist treat her son. She preferred the older family doctor even though he was less qualified. Young preachers have a difficult time gaining the hearing and confidence of the older people. I still have members of the church say, "It's hard for me to listen to what you say because I'm older than you." It takes a while to build up their confidence. But take courage, young preacher, time is on your side!

Personalismo. No other trait has a greater impact upon church management than this characteristic called personalism or *personalismo.* In some circles it is called *caudillismo,* which also helps to explain the trait. The *caudillo* was the large land owner of Latin America, similar to the large cattle ranchers of the West or plantation owners of the South. The *caudillo* was the absolute boss. His word was law, and his will was carried out. He depended upon no one and thus did not cooperate with anybody. The *caudillo* became the hero and status symbol of Latin America.

Personalismo develops into a form of personality struggle.

Men act independently, and it is very difficult to get any two to cooperate fully with one another. I suppose this has been one of the greatest hindrances to democracy in Latin America. If the candidate can't be president, he either starts his own country or shoots the newly elected president. In ecclesiastical matters, the church organization is affected by strong-willed independent men and leaders who cannot cooperate with one another. If they are not the boss, the "big shot" of the church, committee, or organization, they'll have no part of it. Hispanics are not the only ones with this problem (see 3 John 9), but it explains why Hispanic leaders—church leaders included—have such a difficult time getting along.

El corazon. Hispanics are people of the heart. They are very emotional. If something is not from the heart, *el corazon,* or for the heart, then it is hard to accept. They are more emotional than rational, more for feelings than logic. All of culture is permeated with what strikes the heart, not the head alone. A truth wrapped up in cold logic without warmth of life and emotions is not very well received. A half-truth wrapped in emotion may be totally swallowed up. Take for instance the veneration of Mary. They reason thus: "The mother loves the son, and the son loves the mother. If you ask the mother (Mary) to ask the son (Jesus) for something, he will do it." Such reasoning is not logical. It's emotional. We just have to understand the strong bond existing between mother and son.

Some people don't realize how much Roman Catholicism appeals to the emotions. The leaders are called fathers, *padrecitos.* The nuns are called mothers, *madrecitas.* The statues always depict the sufferings of Jesus. Anglos tend to prefer the empty cross that reminds us of our justification. But for Hispanics the crucifix with its suffering Jesus appeals to the heart. The religion is wrapped around the culture, appealing to all the human emotions from baptism (a human love for babies) to death (the sorrow of a parting one). Herein lies the great success of Roman Catholicism among the Latin people.

The Pentecostal movement and the modern Charismatic movement have made great strides among Hispanics because they have been able to capitalize on their emotional natures. Pentecostal churches are characterized by spontaneity and emotional singing and preaching. Healings, exorcisms, being "slain in the Spirit," and the like accompany many of these churches.

RELIGION

We will not say much about the religious heritage of the Hispanic people except to make a few general statements. Much has been written on this subject that can help any person working among them.

Catholic. "Montoya! That's Spanish. You must be a Catholic." And so goes the stereotype. Rightfully so! Most Hispanics are Roman Catholics. Most were baptized into the church and spent their early years in it. They most likely were married in it and their families will call a priest to bury them when they die.

Not all Hispanics are faithful Catholics. In fact, only a small fraction of Hispanics in America are truly loyal church-going Roman Catholics. The churches are rarely filled to capacity on regular Sundays. Most defy the papal declaration against abortions and birth control. Many do not even believe in papal infallibility as a personal creed. They pay lip service to the church and contradict its teachings with their lives. Hispanics in the United States are less conservative and loyal than those in Latin America and thus they are ripe for the gospel.

Culturally integrated. The hold of Catholicism upon the Hispanic is not so much—or even primarily—based on

19

religious belief. It has more to do with how much it has become a part of the culture. A person does not leave the Catholic church without also leaving the culture and a way of life. Every aspect of life is incorporated and integrated into the religion. Births, marriages, rites of puberty, holidays, even names all involve religion. Thus, it is no easy matter for a person to leave the Roman Catholic church. The Christian church must be able to minister to the total person by providing friendships, activities, reorientation, and a clear-cut definition of a Christian. Without that the total conversion will be hard to accomplish.

Maternalistic. Another insight into the religious heritage of Hispanics is that the religious life is dominated by women. The hierarchy of the church is male, but women do the everyday instructing and inspiring. The father in the home is not highly religious. He may make his appearances in church at Easter and Christmas and special occasions, but society does not expect him to be overly religious. The mother or wife is the religious stalwart of the family. She instills faith in her children. She takes them to church. Thus she provides most of the credibility to the veneration of Mary.

Of course, this inability to minister to the total family is an inherent weakness of Roman Catholicism. It lacks the strength which would come from men. The Christian church which fails to win the man for Christ will also develop the same weaknesses. The joy of God's truth and His Word is that it can and does minister to the total family, providing to men their rightful place as the spiritual leaders of their homes.

THE AMERICAN IMPACT

The Hispanic community in America is constantly changing. The greatest factor affecting these changes is the

American way of life. Though the community may try to preserve its language and culture, the American culture is too overbearing. The changes are taking place; some for good and some for bad. Let's look at the impact American culture is making on Hispanic culture.

Spanglish. The mixture of English and Spanish presents some surprising results. The first is a unique form of conversation called "Spanglish," a style of speaking where English and Spanish are intermingled throughout the conversation. Consider this sentence: *"Vengan pacá*, because if you don't, *te voy a pegar!"* You obviously have to be bilingual to catch it all. Or sometimes English words are made into Spanish, like *carro* ("car"), *brekas* ("brakes"), *parquiar* ("to park"). In many cases a form of *barrio* slang develops among the more illiterate and becomes the lingua franca of the community.

Social mobility. Most of Latin America knows only two classes: upper and lower. Wealth is pretty much locked into the hands of the upper class, and few from the lower move into the higher. But America opens up possibilities for change. The poor in Latin America see the United States as a place of opportunity where gold can be swept off the streets. There is hope in America. A person is not doomed to be poor but can rise to a comfortable standard of living through hard work and ingenuity. It's for this reason that Hispanics in America are a generally hardworking and happy people. Social mobility has greatly changed their lives.

Materialism. Of course, the overemphasis in America on wealth and the accumulation of wealth also has an effect upon Hispanics. Normally a fun-loving, pleasant, person-oriented people, they are becoming more materialistic. Traditional values like respect, the family, the strong attachment to emotions, and even faith are being supplanted by the quest for material things.

Family disintegration. Family life in America continues to decline. Divorces equal marriages. Infidelity, homosexuality, feminism all contribute to the breakdown of the traditional American family structure. It is sad to see an Hispanic family immigrate to America and survive all sorts of trouble, only to succumb to America's social ills. Traditional Hispanic family loyalties are giving way to the "modern" way of doing things.

Liberalism. Large denominations have slipped from the "old-time religion" to a new religion powerless to save. We have seen many fine Hispanic ministers suffer at the hands of liberal professors in some of our most distinguished seminaries. With its emphasis on degrees and accreditation, America has lured the most promising Hispanic minds to liberal schools and colleges, where they have either lost their faith entirely or become so tainted with humanistic reasoning that they are useless to their own people.

In spite of all the harmful American influences on Hispanic culture, I feel we have the best to offer them: the hope in Jesus Christ. America is still the bastion of Christianity, the well of water for the spiritually thirsty billions of the world. God has sovereignly brought millions to its shores and cities, and now America has another chance to feed them the Bread of Life and to give them the Water of Life. My prayer is that the following chapters will challenge many to devote their energies to this sacred task and to help others carry out this task to the glory of God. The Hispanic world may be different, but God can save Hispanics, and He can do it through us.

2

The Hispanic Pastor

> For this reason I left you in Crete, that you might set in
> order what remains, and appoint elders in every city as I
> directed you, namely, if any man be above reproach . . .
> (*Titus 1:5–6*).

So much of what is done in the church depends upon its
leadership, namely, the pastor or missionary. The key
ingredient, aside from God's sovereign hand, is leadership.
If God does not raise up committed leadership for the
Hispanic community, I fear all will be lost. The purpose of
this chapter is to show the kind of leader we ought to have in
our communities.

Anglo-American Christians may not understand the importance of this chapter since they are not experiencing a
leadership lag or gap. In fact, we may almost say that
America has a surplus of Christian leaders. They may not all
be excellent, but at least they have a measure of competence.

The Hispanic Christian community does not have such a
surplus, nor is there even an adequate number to minister to
the existing community. Churches go for years with lay
leadership or with ministers who pastor two or three
churches at one time. Add to that the poor educational
preparation most of them have, and you can begin to sense
our frustration. A quick glance at our seminaries and Bible
colleges shows a lack of Hispanic enrollees. Our future looks
bleak. But I am still optimistic. I do not believe the work will

be done by Hispanics alone. Nor do I think that these masses will be won to Christ through established North American patterns of church growth.

THE FALSE ASSUMPTIONS

Let me begin by addressing our Anglo-American brethren. The devil has sown much propaganda about how impossible it is for Anglos to reach Hispanics for Christ, and many churches and church leaders have bought that lie. It *is* possible for Anglos to reach Hispanics for Christ. I do not say it is easy, but it is possible. I was led to Christ by an Anglo missionary in my hometown and discipled by an Anglo evangelist, Billy Graham. Anglo-Americans must be open to God's power to use them to minister to Hispanics. We need their help in planting and pastoring Hispanic churches.

"I'm not their kind." The first lie Satan throws out is that you're not their kind. They're Hispanics, and you're an Anglo. They are brown, you are white. They speak Spanish, you speak English. We have been so brainwashed by segregationists and prejudiced people that even some well-meaning Christians speak of "different races." But we must keep in mind that there is only one race, the human race. We are all fundamentally of "the same kind." If we find the means to communicate and if we try, we can communicate.

"They won't accept me." Satan may also discourage the Anglo missionary or pastor by putting this phrase into his head: "You're Anglo. Hispanics can never accept you." That is a lie. Two of my dearest friends are Anglo pastors, and they both pastor predominantly Hispanic congregations. Hispanics *will* accept Anglo pastors. They accept Anglo presidents, governors, mayors, doctors, teachers, bankers, day-care center directors, so why not Anglo pastors?
The secret to the Hispanic accepting the Anglo is for the

Anglo to accept Hispanics to the point where he almost forgets that he is Anglo and they Hispanic.

A leading magazine ran a true story of a mother who told her daughter, "You have the eyes of your father."

The next day the daughter told her mother, "Mom, yesterday you paid me the greatest compliment of my life. You said I have my father's eyes, and you and dad aren't my real parents. You adopted me!"

"Oh, that's right," said the mother. "I had forgotten."

That is the way an Anglo pastor should look at his Hispanic community. He should forget he is Anglo. They should become his people.

People of other nationalities will accept us if they see in us a genuine attitude of acceptance. In a home Bible study I was conducting, our discussion turned to racial distinctions and the efforts made to reach beyond them. One dear man whom I led to Christ, an Anglo, said, "I trust you more with my soul than I do any Anglo minister." That was a real compliment to me, not in my abilities to minister, but as proof of my ability to see all people the same. There can be and will be an acceptance by Hispanics of Anglo ministers and vice versa.

"God works better through their kind." We have often heard that statement. In other words, God can more easily reach people through others from their own nationality, economic status, and cultural background. There is no disputing the argument. People are more readily won by people of their own kind.

But that doesn't mean God is limited to working only within such cultural boundaries. All it means is that people who share a culture have already established a natural means of communication. We will speak more about this tremendous truth in chapter 4 ("Indigenous Principles at Work").

Yet we must be perfectly candid and at least biblical. God reached the Ninevites through Jonah who wasn't "their kind." He wasn't even willing to accept them. Jesus reached the woman at the well who wasn't "His kind." In all missionary activity there is going to be that cross-cultural step taken to introduce the gospel to a people not of "our kind." It may be easier for those of the "same kind" to do evangelism and ministry, but if these messengers do not exist, then others of a "different kind" must be willing to introduce the gospel.

The bottom line is this. If those of the "same kind" are not doing it, then those of a different kind *must* do it. The disciples were told to spread the gospel to all kinds, not just to their kind (Acts 1:8). We must never shy away from a scriptural mandate to accommodate a missionary method. God blesses obedience, not logic. We must dare to do the difficult that others may do what is easier. It may be more difficult to do cross-cultural ministry, but intercultural ministry will not take place without it. Do it if you have to.

"They don't need us." The Third World is coming of age, but even they cannot exist without Western assistance. In the area of missions, we have often sensed that the world does not need missionaries, especially English-speaking missionaries. So some may reason, "Hispanics do not need Anglo missionaries. They have enough pastors and laymen to do the task." Such reasoning is based upon a wrong analysis of the state of the Hispanic church. In the Los Angeles basin, less than 5 percent of the Hispanic population is evangelical or "born again." This small group of Hispanic Christians can use all the help it can get.

Every assistance offered to the Hispanic community speeds up the process of evangelization and discipleship. When our church was running seventy-five to a hundred in attendance, we had a summer program where forty to sixty members of the Navigators came to minister to us for six weeks. They lived with our people, conducted Bible studies, and discipled as they knew how. In six weeks, fifty students, almost all Anglos, accomplished what would take our staff from six months to a year. Did we need them? Yes, indeed!

The Hispanic church will always need the Anglo church. The relationships may change from decade to decade, but there will always be an interdependence between them. The Liberation Theology of Latin America is political and economic in nature, but the true liberation theology of the Bible makes us one and part of the same body. We can never totally reject the rest of the body. We are forever wedded to one another, and someday, thanks to our Anglo brethren, the Anglo masses may receive missionaries from their southern neighbors.

In short, no one should discourage a feeling or turn down a call to serve other people who are not of the same ethnic background. If God calls you, then He will use you. If you sincerely love these people, you will do them much good. In comparison to labors at home or the work of their own kind, it may not seem like much; but we must remember that in the kingdom of God *every soul counts.*

THE INDISPENSABLE INGREDIENTS

I would like to focus my attention on the missionary-pastor and show the ingredients present in his or her life. It takes a certain kind of person to minister to Hispanics. They're not an exclusive bunch, but certain qualities should be present. A list of qualities necessary for spiritual leadership can be found in 1 Timothy 3:1–8. I simply want to add or emphasize those which are indispensable for success in church planting.

Spiritually minded. The pastor or missionary must be full of Christ. Those not possessing a vibrant relationship with our Lord Jesus will find the task much too heavy and their lives much too weak. Some workers have been more concerned about their academic degrees, housing expenses, and the like than about the reality of Christ and the imminent damnation of these precious souls. Even Hispanic pastors leave the precious task of soul winning to pursue higher degrees which do nothing for their spiritual vitality and drain their energies from the harvest fields. I have come to realize that the average Hispanic on the street cares nothing for my academic degrees. He wants only to know of my God. May we not fail him.

Hispanics expect more from the Christian worker than what they were offered in their native religions. A close walk with God, free of worldliness and trivia, is a necessity, nay, an imperative. We don't need more experts devoid of Christ. We don't need moral washouts. We need men and women in love with Jesus and anxious to make Him known.

Unprejudiced. Men of bigotry are not wanted, and will not succeed among Hispanics. This even includes Hispanics. For there are some men in Hispanic pulpits full of prejudice and bigotry toward people of other nationalities. Such men are odious to the sacred task and doomed to write "Ichabod" across the doors of their churches. Prejudice carries with it a stench strong enough to drive away the faithful, leaving behind the baser sort incapable of reaching others outside themselves. Only as we see people as needy as ourselves can we labor for them as we ought. The Hispanic pastor or missionary must have a heart free from subtle prejudices.

Adaptable. I once read a book by Robert Girard entitled, *Brethren, Hang Loose!* That could serve as a motto for workers among Hispanics. They must be adaptable to language and customs. The desert lizard survives its harsh environment because it can so readily adapt itself to its surroundings. We must learn to do the same. For some there is a language to be learned. They must try not to lose heart; nor should they feel embarrassed. Even Hispanics need to learn Spanish and should not shy from it. At times I begin my Spanish sermons with a slight apology for my lack of expertise in the language. Yet, the people are always so eager to help me when I am at a loss for words. At one time I was afraid and ashamed, now we laugh together and they help me when I'm stuck.

Ruth said, "Your people shall be my people" (Ruth 1:16), and that must be your attitude too. Things won't always be done the way they were back home or in your home church. You must learn their ways. You must even learn to eat their food. (You haven't really lived until you've tried tacos, *menudo*, and *tripas*.)

Experienced and prepared. The pastorate has never been a place for novices, much less the mission field. Yet I have been appalled at churches' willingness to commission men and women for foreign missions whom they would not have serve in their own churches. Those who serve among Hispanics need to know what they are doing. I would recommend a one- or two-year internship in some church, with emphasis on soul winning, discipling, and family counseling. Those who go out to specialize in church planting should have at least started or pastored a church. A few years spent in training are well worth the time and energy. Thoroughness and excellence are two qualities for which we must all strive.

Young people shouldn't expect to be able to go directly from seminary or Bible school to the field and be successful. I have seen numerous young men fail miserably in their pastorates or efforts at cross-cultural ministry. In most of these cases they had little or no practical experience in ministering. They expected to sail on the wind of educational achievements. A grass roots ministry is mostly a practical ministry with little emphasis on the theoretical. Hence we must be as practically prepared as possible.

Patient. Hispanics are both a suspicious and emotional people, which makes for a frustrating and discouraging work. They may linger a long time before they fully accept the things we are saying or doing. Their distrust of youth may prove to be a discouraging factor to a young minister wanting to see results overnight. Unless he is patient, he may be tempted to quit too soon or become enraged at the people for not responding as they should. Anglo missionaries must exercise great patience as they work to gain a confidence and a suitable hearing.

At the same time, Hispanics are an emotional and accommodating people, acting upon their emotions without a true commitment. Hispanics like to please. They may tell you what you want to hear and then not follow through. They may profess to accept Christ or promise to come to church, then not show up. You can't really get mad at them. It's just their sweet way of telling you "no thanks" without hurting your feelings. This calls for all the Christian patience available.

Shrewd and harmless. Jesus once told His disciples, "Be shrewd as serpents, and innocent as doves" (Matthew 10:16). My advice to you who work among Hispanics is the same: Be shrewd! We must always keep in mind that we are dealing with a basic non-Christian populace, where poverty, ignorance, and crime are ways of life for some. I have had young drug addicts come to me with heartbreaking sob stories. If I had not been shrewd, they would have taken my clothes. One lady made her living by going from church to church asking for money. She "burned" me once, but not twice.

In the *barrios* the young militants and revolutionaries try to intimidate and even blackmail you—and will if you let them. In one case they persuaded a denomination to turn over a church in the *barrio* to them, which they subsequently turned into a center for revolutionary activity. The last I saw of it, it had been burned down and was demolished for a parking lot! What a waste of the Lord's property. We must learn not to be intimidated by such blatant antagonism to the gospel.

At the same time the minister must keep from becoming cynical and bitter. Love must reign supreme in our hearts. The only way the Aucas of Ecuador could be won was by missionaries like Elisabeth Elliot, who refused to become bitter over evil activities, even the murder of her husband Jim. Things will happen to us which would drive others away. But real love and gentleness will keep us working. At times we might be tempted to strike back, but gentleness is the better way. A father of a young girl called me to complain of his daughter's conversion to "this religion." At times he was almost insulting, yet I tried to be patient and loving to him. God later gave me the blessed privilege of leading him to Christ. God can melt these hearts of stone.

SOME DIFFICULTIES

What I have to say in the following paragraphs pertains especially to pastors of Hispanic churches and not specifically to missionaries to the Hispanics. Hispanic pastors will encounter a number of difficulties in their ministries and congregations. It is well that one know some of these before he puts his hand to the plow, lest he look back and become unfit for the kingdom of God. I have personally encountered most of those difficulties and by God's grace have endured them.

Poverty. The Hispanic community is by and large a poor community by American standards. No pastor should consider this ministry with an eye toward the accumulation of wealth or attaining more than a comfortable standard of living. One must resolve this question long before he embarks along this trail, otherwise he will always be longing for the spoils of Egypt.

Our starting salary in 1972 was two hundred dollars a month. It was for full-time work and was supposed to feed and house a family of three. That was all the church could afford; yet, it was enough for us. For a man with four years of college and three years of postgraduate study, it didn't seem proper remuneration. But one must realize that an Hispanic church will rarely be able to compensate the labor of the minister in money. His compensation will come in souls and in heavenly crowns.

The Hispanic minister and his family will find themselves living like most of the parishioners. If they drive used cars, so will he. If they frequent secondhand stores, so will he. If they cannot afford the luxuries of life, neither will he. If they are deprived of many material things, so will he be! Some men have left much behind to serve God's people, and in almost every case God has replaced what they left behind with more satisfying things.

The minister will have to find some way to make ends meet. Some ministers take the unfortunate course of becoming part-time ministers as they work full time in some secular employment not related to their ministry. The result is obvious: a part-time church. Building a church is like building a business. You have to put all your time and heart into it. I have already mentioned how my church could only pay two hundred dollars a month. I knew that God could raise a church there and that if I devoted all my energies to soul winning and ministering, there would soon be a church large enough to support my family. My own guideline is, "If a man cannot get enough people saved in six months to support him, he is not doing his job and has no business pastoring a church." Moreover, ministers who put their wives to work are also doing their congregations and themselves a great disservice. The wife should be free to minister to her husband and to help the women of the church.

I believe in "tent making," as illustrated by the apostle Paul, but only as a means to an end. A minister may be temporarily employed to build up enough cash reserves to allow him to work full-time at his ministry. The way to beat the poverty in our churches is through the dedicated ministry of a man to a people. The people will be more committed and the church will be larger. Within two years, we saw a tiny congregation grow to where it could support two full-time workers. Proverbs 27:23 says, "Know well the condition of your flocks, / And pay attention to your herds." Verses 24–27 relate the rewards of a diligent pastor.

Ignorance. Many Hispanics do not read well. Many never finished school. Still others do not have the benefit of well-educated parents. Nor are their environments the most advanced. Even simple truths are veiled in darkness. All these can frustrate a zealous preacher.

If a minister can be realistic and patient, and if he can implement a number of educational programs for his church, he can quickly alter the condition of his people. The gospel naturally lifts. People who cannot read or write are converted, and soon they are motivated to read the Bible and to write. Upon coming to East Los Angeles, I quickly abandoned the King James Version in favor of the New American Standard Bible because the people just couldn't understand the text. We sometimes start them on the Good News Bible or the Living Bible and then wean them as soon as possible to a more literal translation of the Scriptures.

Hispanics are a proud people and easily embarrassed, especially men. Therefore, we cannot always use conventional teaching methods like recitation or role playing which might reveal their ignorance. One man refused to go to Sunday school for fear of being called on to read. We must have a great deal of sanctified common sense. Nor should we ever give them the impression that we are so learned and they so ignorant. One man continually addressed his audience as "you people" and accentuated the educational gulf between himself and them. As the gulf grew, the audience shrank. They might have been ignorant, but they weren't stupid!

Ungodliness. The hardest aspect of the ministry to accept is the extreme depravity of our people. Because they are sinful, the gospel is extremely Good News. But, because so many are so sinful, backsliding can be devastating. In an

Anglo community, where people are raised in "churchianity," backsliding may amount to simply not attending church or not supporting the programs. Among Hispanics, where drunkenness is rampant, immorality great, poverty abundant, and families large, backsliding is a fearful phenomenon. We may take a father of four or five children, save him from drunkenness, get him a job, disciple his children, and then after all those hours spent on one man, he can backslide and lose his job and stability. It can happen again and again. It is tempting to stop trying.

A typical church will be filled with large families, single-parent families on welfare, ex-addicts, young people without adequate education, and the smell of the world right at the church door. What kind of minister is equal to the challenge? Yet God can make us adequate!

Pulpits in these churches cannot be devoted to unfolding the niceties of the tabernacle or pouring out pious statements on social order. They must deal with the problem of sin. Otherwise, they are worthless physicians who seek only to alleviate the physical sufferings of the people but who don't care about or do anything to cure the cause. Souls must be anointed with healing from the Son of Righteousness.

Divisions. What pastor is there who is not concerned about internal strife and divisions? May I add that lower-class communities are open territory for all sorts of cults and false teachings. We have seen every conceivable form of false teaching available, and at times it has even threatened to enter the church. Many pastors have labored for years only to see their churches split over some disagreement on doctrine or policy or to have the church down the street take its members.

There is no easy remedy for a division. If it should come over doctrine, the best remedy is a clearly defined statement of faith and the indoctrination of all members in what the church believes. We should never apologize for believing in something. Strong teaching of doctrine does not divide, it unites. If the problem should be over personality conflicts, the problem can be resolved and avoided by a strong, competent, compassionate pastor, who can be lovingly forceful when he has to be. There is enough room in the community to start new churches without some Diotrephes wanting to split the church. Best send him on his way with his half-dozen followers to start their own church. If they succeed, praise God! Now you have two gospel stations. If they fail, praise God anyway!

As to the problem of "sheep stealing" and proselytizing, I would say, do not practice this unchristian practice yourself, and God will not visit your heads with the same malady. I have made it a practice never to visit a member of a neighboring church, nor will I counsel another member without their pastor's consent. I never preach to draw other Christians, but rather to convert and strengthen those God brings me. Also, if we provide a warm, loving, exciting church, people will not be attracted to other churches. I don't preach that my people not visit other churches. I let them visit all they want. But they do hear of all they missed when they weren't with us, and then they usually will not want to miss again. Build loyalty in the people by being loyal to them. Mind the customer and he will be back for more.

I have endeavored to share a few practical insights on the Hispanic pastor as I see him. He must be most Christ-like in his motives, "For you know the grace of our Lord Jesus Christ, that though he was rich, yet for your sake He became poor, that you through His poverty might become rich" (2 Corinthians 8:9). Surely no one can decry a man for wanting to enrich another's life! It will be said of him as was said of a certain one, "He is worthy for You to grant this to him; for he loves our nation, and it was he who built us our synagogue" (Luke 7:4–5).

3

Effective Evangelism

And every day, in the temple and from house to house,
they kept right on teaching and preaching Jesus as the
Christ (Acts 5:42).

The key word for the Hispanic church is "evangelism." The
Hispanic population in America has increased by 60 percent
over the last decade, yet less than 10 percent is Christian.
Winning the lost has to be our chief objective. This chapter
will deal with effective evangelism: its message, its method,
and the mobilization of the church for it.

An Effective Gospel. Let me state clearly that it is the
gospel which saves, not any of man's ideas or clever
methods: "For I am not ashamed of the gospel, for it is the
power of God for salvation to every one who believes, to the
Jew first and also to the Greek" (Romans 1:16). The pure
gospel as Paul gives it is "That Christ died for our sins
according to the Scriptures, and that He was buried, and that
He was raised on the third day according to the Scriptures"
(1 Corinthians 15:3–4). Much preaching today is not gospel
preaching, so we should not wonder at the meager results.

Anglo preachers have a tendency to water down the gospel
for fear of offending Hispanics or because they're more
concerned with church growth than true conversion. But
Hispanics—given their Roman Catholic background—des-
perately need to hear the true gospel. Those who wish to see

true conversions among them must become accustomed to preaching a true and effective gospel.

Saving gospel, not social. The Hispanic needs to be saved, not improved. What good does it do if we take the man out of the *barrio* if we do not save him from hell? The social gospel has done little more than put a Band-Aid upon a deadly wound. We may preach to man's hurts and teach him to deal with his environment, but if we do not teach him of God, he will never probe the root cause of his misery.

Many other methods have been substituted for gospel preaching. Some go out from house to house inviting people to visit (or even join) the church. That is not gospel preaching. Preachers get in their pulpits and preach church membership, attendance, tithing, and even holy living. That is not gospel preaching. The problem with many preachers is that they aim too low. They want the people to come to their church to join their churches and denominations. We need to preach so men and women join God's church, whether or not they come to our door.

When we send our people out to do door-to-door evangelism, I strictly enforce this principle. "We are not there to socialize. We are not there to invite them back. We are not after their money. We are after their souls. We want to know if they know Jesus Christ as their personal Savior and are trusting Him alone for salvation. We will not leave until we have adequately shared the substitutionary death of the God-man for a totally depraved world and until we have given them an opportunity to repent and receive Jesus into their lives. If we have not done that, we have not preached the gospel." Preach to convert a sinner into heaven and not to gain a member for your church.

Evangelical, not ecumenical. The gospel is very pointed, and especially clear. Yet we see a movement today to make the gospel ecumenical and not evangelical. Although we are preaching to mostly Roman Catholics, we cannot and dare not commit the grievous error of accepting the Roman Catholic gospel as the real gospel. The true gospel of Jesus Christ when it sincerely touches the life of a man will make him turn from his wicked ways, and we must go as far as to include the system of false teaching found in Roman Catholicism.

No one likes to be tricked into something. Evangelical preaching clearly shows the vast difference between the gospel of grace found in Scripture and the system of works found in Catholicism. Paul called the system of works "a different gospel," one which also damns (Galatians 1:6, 9). We have an obligation to show the clear-cut differences between Catholic teachings and the true gospel. We also never attack Catholic people, only the system. This method yields marvelous results, and the converts have been solid and zealous for the truth.

True, not theatrical. Gospel preaching, especially from pulpits, has a tendency to become theatrical if the preacher is after visible results. Some use emotional appeals and scare tactics to draw the soul upward. God have mercy upon us if we exchange heart saving for hand clapping and head counting. These things in themselves are not wrong, but unless sin, sentence of hell, substitutionary atonement, and simple faith are preached, all else fails. Let us preach to save men for eternity.

AN EFFECTIVE METHODOLOGY

People are quick to latch on to methods as inspired by God or reject them as useless and ineffective. My own motto is: Use what works to save souls without compromising the purity of the gospel or God's people. Fishing for men is like fishing for fish: use whatever method you can find and as many as you can find. Paul said, "That I may by all means save some" (1 Corinthians 9:22). The following are some methods that God has blessed in the salvation of souls. You may wish to use them, alter them, or use methods of your own which God has given you. In the *barrio* we say, *todo se vale!* ("Anything is good!")

Personal evangelism. Peter said, "Always being ready to make a defense to every one who asks you to give an account for the hope that is in you" (1 Peter 3:15), and Paul said, "Preach the word; be ready in season and out of season" (2 Timothy 4:2). The pastor must be an active, personal soul winner. He must know how to deal with souls. I must always keep in mind that God did not bring me to East Los Angeles primarily to pastor a church, but to win souls. Yet often I have fallen into the trap of maintaining the church and not advancing the cause of the gospel. Here is the greatest key to effective evangelism: a man of God set aflame with the gospel of grace.

Pulpit evangelism. Hispanic preachers must be able to preach the gospel effectively from the pulpit to the pew. North American churches have pretty well settled into the role of discipleship or expository preaching. Pulpit thunder is now relegated to social issues. The evangelistic meeting and service have pretty much died down to nothing. Evangelism has taken other forms, but the pulpit is not one of those forms.

The situation in the Hispanic church is much different. It is at the point today where the Anglo church was in the days of Moody. Then the pulpits were ablaze with gospel preachers. Today Hispanics are breaking loose from the Roman Catholic Church and are attending Protestant gatherings in unprecedented numbers. The need for clear gospel preaching in our churches is great.

In almost every sermon I preach, the gospel becomes the climax of the message with an invitation offered to anxious hearts to believe in the shed blood of Christ. The Sunday morning services have been especially fruitful. For over ten years I have made it a point to preach from the four Gospels. Visitors have always been present, and hundreds of decisions have been made. Our people invite their unsaved friends to this service, and we try not to disappoint their zeal for the Lord. Everything is centered around the unsaved person.

Let me state clearly that the gospel is not the topic exclusively. There is naturally some truth to help the believers grow and mature in the faith. But although I may preach on prayer, witnessing, hospitality, or election, the message or sermon always ends with a strong, planned appeal to the unsaved. The presentation of the gospel must be planned and never left to chance or sabbatical zeal. Hispanic preachers graduating from some of our institutions of higher learning must be careful not to fall into simple instruction without reaping a harvest of souls. Preach the gospel from your pulpits without fear, compromise, or embarrassment.

Friendship evangelism. The selling feature of Hispanics is their friendliness and tightly knit social structure. Life is a family affair. Hence, evangelism becomes a family affair, a matter of one member of the family sharing with another member of the family or one friend with another. We call it friendship evangelism.

Almost everyone in our church is related to someone else or is a close friend of someone. Very few people ever come into the church services merely out of curiosity. Hispanics do not look in the Yellow Pages for a good Bible-teaching church to attend. More than 90 percent of our visitors come because someone else invited them to come. They get interested in Christ because someone else introduced them to the gospel. Therefore we strive hard to encourage the new Christians to share their newfound faith with all their family and also to invite them to come to the church services. The response has been astounding. One new Christian can, in a span of one month, invite dozens of people to church.

Literature evangelism. "He who sows sparingly shall also reap sparingly" is a vital truth in evangelism. The wise use of good gospel literature is an excellent means to promote the gospel and your church. Investing money for the purchase of gospel tracts can be the best means to win a soul to Christ. It also furnishes ammunition for the new Christian who has difficulty sharing his faith.

We have had to print many of our own gospel tracts because the quality and relevancy of others were not up to par. They may be good in other areas, but we needed something more to the point. In the *barrio,* we have used *"El Perdido," "Mi Vida Loca," "Tu Placaso,"* "Illegal Alien," and "The Three Crosses" with great success. We have used thousands of these to cover the entire community.

Tract racks should be placed in convenient locations where the believers can pick up gospel tracts, put them in their purses or pockets, and put them to good use throughout the week. We have had some of them returned in the mail without stamps with people's names on them. Every serious church should invest time and money in literature evangelism.

Thousands of Gospels of John are distributed every year. Every person who makes a decision for Christ is given one. The simple Word of God works wonders upon the hearts of people. Just make sure you use a simple, readable version of the gospel.

Film evangelism. We discovered another effective method of evangelism by accident. Others may have been aware of it, but to us at least, it was a remarkable discovery. One of our young men had been killed in a gang-related slaying, and the church decided to begin a film ministry on Friday nights to keep the kids off the streets and provide a place to gather. Soon we found that hundreds of people would flock to film night to see Christian films, and scores were getting saved by them. Our greatest number of recorded decisions for Christ have come through the showing of gospel films.

Our church has invested hundreds of dollars in equipment, personnel, and films for this program, and not one cent has been a waste of the Lord's money. Films like *The Burning Hell, A Thief in the Night, A Distant Thunder, The Beast, All the King's Horses, Night Son,* and a host of others are powerful ways to present the gospel. Many Hispanics who will not go to church to hear a preacher will go to see a film.

Children-youth evangelism. The typical patterns of Child Evangelism classes, vacation Bible school, and children's ministry are fruitful ways to present the gospel. We also operate a bus ministry into five housing projects with great success in spite of the youthfulness of our workers and expensiveness of the program. A bus ministry, when prayerfully executed, will yield any church great results.

Recently we began lunch-hour Bible classes at the local high schools with great success. Up to two hundred students at one time have attended these classes which are no more than evangelistic rallies. The young people are open to the gospel and respond with great enthusiasm. We find a leader, get permission from the school, arrange for a teacher to act as sponsor, begin with a nucleus of kids, and away we go to a great harvest of souls.

House-to-house evangelism. The simple method of door knocking should not be avoided. In our church we have developed a program of personal evangelism called the WIN Program. I will describe this program later in the chapter. At this point let me simply emphasize the importance of house-to-house visitation. When all else fails, go from house to house. It is the New Testament method (Acts 5:42).

Park evangelism. Hispanics, because of their poverty and love for the outdoors, delight to congregate at local parks. Hence a good park ministry is an excellent way to gather in more fruit. A park team may consist of a musical group, a half-dozen counselors, and a couple of open-air preachers. Select a well-populated park, sing a few songs to gather a crowd, introduce a couple of people with exciting testimonies, and then give a short evangelistic message followed by an appeal to make a decision for Christ. The rest of the team can disperse after the message to share one-to-one with the curious and the ones seeking Christ.

Wedding-funeral evangelism. The religious nature of the Hispanic culture and the newness of the gospel message provide an open door in two of the most popular social gatherings of the Hispanic: weddings and funerals.

We have used the Christian wedding as a beautiful way to introduce the gospel. Often the young couple have unsaved parents or a host of unsaved relatives. It is impolite in Hispanic circles to turn down an invitation to a wedding, no matter where it is, and it's much worse for the relatives not to be invited. Hence, early in my ministry, I resolved to preach a full-length gospel message at every wedding I performed. The results have been more than gratifying. We also endeavor to have a reception where Christ is magnified, where Christians mingle with non-Christians, and where Christian precepts and principles are shared.

The funeral is also an opportune time for such preaching of the gospel. More difficult than the wedding, it still provides an excellent means to minister the Word of God. Just recently I was called upon to participate in a funeral in a Catholic church for a little girl who had burned to death. I followed the saying of the rosary and had an excellent opportunity to preach the glorious gospel. When people are hurting because of a loss in the family, we can surely show mercy and give a word of hope. Funerals for unsaved people are difficult, but we can minister to the living and leave it to God to judge the dead. Focus on the family and friends, and God will give you open hearts.

Take any and all of these methods and use them for the gospel's sake. If God be pleased to use even one, your labor will not be in vain, and you will be rejoicing along with the angels in heaven.

AN EFFECTIVE CONSERVATION

In the Lord's teaching on the four soils, He mentions one which bears fruit in varying degrees of productivity, whereas the other three abort the seed and render the planting fruitless (Matthew 13:18–23). Gospel preaching follows the same pattern. Every evangelist desires every professed convert to proceed to maturity and yield fruit "some a hundredfold, some sixty, and some thirty" (Matthew 13:23). Christ taught us such would not be the case. Many would be professors of a new life but not actual possessors of a new life (John 2:23–25; 6:64, 66).

Bearing this reality in mind—for no preacher of the gospel can sanely continue in ministry unless he does—there are certain steps the shepherd can take to foster the maturity of believers and to help identify the true believers. Much fruit is lost through poor methods of conservation. It is true that the sovereign God loses none of His children regardless of how ineffective our methods might be (see John 6:39; 10:26–29; 1 Corinthians 3:6–9; Philippians 1:6). Yet we have been commanded by the Chief Shepherd to so shepherd His flock that none may be lost to the cares of the flesh and the snare of evildoers (Acts 20:28–31; 1 Peter 5:1–4).

We offer then a few simple guidelines to help such careful shepherds who desire real blessedness for the souls they are used of God to save and who desire the joy of ministering to large and growing congregations. More of our churches would increase in number and strength if the pastors would take steps to plug the holes in their ministries.

The call for decisions. We are heirs to the methodologies of the evangelists of North America, namely, Finney, Moody, Sunday, and Graham. Each of them was used mightily of

God for the harvesting of His vineyard, and able harvesters they were. One thing they all had in common was the pressing of the individual for a decision concerning Christ. From Finney to Graham, each developed his unique method of calling forth for public decisions. Whereas in times past, anxious inquirers had been left to ponder this momentous decision, these men provided means by which inquirers and seekers could receive help in coming to a decision or guidance subsequent to their belief in Christ.

The call for decisions is both biblical and practical. The Lord called men and women publicly to follow after him (Matthew 4:18–22; 8:18–22; 9:9). The apostles did no less than to call people to a decision (Acts 2:36–41; 8:30–39). The exact manner in which this is to be done is not laid down for us in Scripture. If the decision to receive Christ is an individual decision, if it is based on the Spirit's prompting, and if it is based on an act of the will responding in faith, then it would seem that we have just cause to ask for an individual public profession or decision to receive Christ as Savior (see Mark 10:17–22; John 6:44; Acts 16:31–33; Ephesians 2:8–9).

The invitation to accept or receive Christ (John 1:12) should be a simple, direct, honest, and sacred invitation. A pastor should invite people personally to believe in Jesus and appeal to the will for that decision. A pastor should personally lead men and women to Christ every year. He can extend the same invitation to a large gathering by addressing himself to those present who have not yet made that decision. The call may be by the raising of hands, standing up, coming to the front of the church, meeting with him after the service, or joining a counselor in a special room designed for that purpose. Whatever method is used, we encourage every preacher to press for decisions. Many potential converts and church members are lost at this point.

The counseling room. Inquirers should be dealt with concerning their decision to receive Christ. As a young man,

I went forward numerous times in response to invitations, but no one effectively dealt with me about my soul. I might have been spared a lot of confusion and heartache if someone had counseled with me to assure me of my salvation.

We recommend a special room set aside to counsel all who decide for Christ. These rooms should be staffed by conscientious, sensitive soul winners. We have found "New Life in Christ" classes helpful in conserving these results of gospel preaching. We cover key topics beneficial to new believers like "Assurance of Salvation," "Victory Over Sin," "How to Pray," "Reading God's Word," and "Who Is Christ?" The classes also provide a place for them to ask questions about their newfound faith. Ignorance is a great obstacle to faith. Unless their questions are dealt with, they may not grow in Christ as they should.

New believers need special attention just as newborn babes do. The whole church needs to be sensitive to their needs and should work together to help them grow in the Lord. Sunday school teachers and preachers should not teach above their heads. Great tolerance needs to be exercised in their formative weeks.

Our "New Life in Christ" classes meet in the best rooms in the church and are taught by the finest men. They meet twice a week; an hour before the Sunday evening service and then again on Tuesday evening. The classes are four weeks long, and a new class begins every week. Thus those who begin the class together continue for four weeks without interruptions by new people coming in. At the end of four weeks we hold a baptismal service for those who desire to be baptized into Christ.

The commitment to baptism. Jesus made baptism an important part of a disciple's life (Matthew 28:19–20; see also Acts 2:38–41). Though baptism is not a prerequisite for salvation (see Mark 16:16; 1 Corinthians 1:13–14), it is the way of identifying those who have made a decision to become Christians. Hispanics place a greater emphasis on baptism than do the Anglo churches as a whole. Hispanics view baptism as the one proof of relinquishing all ties with their old religions and with a sinful way of life.

The church would do well to continue such an emphasis, with great care not to confuse baptism with salvation or to teach baptismal regeneration. Baptism can serve as the rallying point for both new convert and church alike. We make the day of baptism a great day in the life of our church. There is a dinner held for those to be baptized. They are encouraged to invite all their friends and family to the special service. Each of them gives a testimony just before being immersed in water. Then the clear gospel is preached, and the newly baptized receive a beautiful baptismal certificate, after which the whole congregation congratulates them. The day is a festive and holy occasion.

Church membership. After the new believer is baptized, he is not immediately ushered into the membership of our church. It is true that he is already a part of the body of Christ the very moment he is born again (John 3:3-5; 1 Corinthians 12:13). And it is also true that many who do not belong to any church will be in heaven because of their faith in Christ. But the ideal is to be enrolled in both the visible and the invisible church. And we lead new believers in that direction.

The next step for the newly baptized believer is to enroll in the new members' class. In this twelve-week class the new believer is introduced to the main body of church doctrine covering all the major areas of systematic theology. In this class, they are taught about inspiration, the Trinity, the finished work of Christ, angels and demons, the ministry of the Spirit, the church and its ordinances, the organization and administration of the church, the use of the gifts of the Spirit, biblical tithing and giving, and church discipline, as well as numerous other biblical doctrines.

This mini-course in theology and church policy brings

them up to par with the average member of the church and gives them a chance to minister in the body. Each new member is also given a brief interview with the church elders to insure the church of their salvation and their heart's desire to serve God. The results of this method have been gratifying to our church and a great blessing to our new Christians. Blessed is that church which takes care of Christ's flock.

AN EFFECTIVE MOBILIZATION

Someone said the rate of growth of any movement is in direct proportion to the number of its adherents who are spreading its teaching. The same principle applies to the Christian church. The local church will grow in proportion to the number of church members it has spreading the gospel. We aim to mobilize the whole church membership in evangelism, for when we scatter everywhere, we reach many more with the gospel (see Acts 8:1, 4). In many churches the work of evangelism is left up to the pastor or a few gifted men. The average Christian never deals with souls, and sad to say, doesn't even know how to lead a person to Christ. Your church will grow if you take heed to the following recommendations.

Instill every-person evangelism. The most exciting part of the Christian life next to fellowship with Jesus is leading a lost soul into the kingdom of God. A pastor may forget to share this blessing with the rest of his church, and that would be a terrible crime. It is my firm conviction that every Christian should share the gospel as part of his Christian life. Evangelism is not a gift. Evangelism is a command (see Matthew 28:18–20). God expects all His children to be involved in the proclamation of His gospel. The whole church—pastor and congregation—is responsible for evangelism.

49

One may ask, "How does a pastor instill this into his congregation?" We do it by preaching it from the pulpit as often as needed, and by teaching it to smaller groups at every opportunity. After a while the people will know where you stand on this issue and will eventually follow their beloved shepherd. Most Christians have a natural hesitation to win souls, but if they are taught right, they will eventually receive the boldness through prayer and venture out into the deeper waters of evangelism.

Teach everyone to evangelize. Once the congregation is persuaded to become a part of the evangelistic arm of the church, they must be taught how to evangelize. In our church, we developed a program on soul winning patterned after the Evangelism Explosion method of Coral Ridge Presbyterian Church in Florida. We call it the WIN Program (Witness in the Neighborhood). In a series of classes, we teach the individual Christian how to share his faith under any circumstances.

It is not so much the method that matters as the fact that we have a program that equips every Christian to share his faith. Over 80 percent of our members have completed the course in personal soul winning. A program in evangelistic instruction is equal in importance to a Sunday school class. It is critical to the overall growth of the church and may be the one factor responsible for church growth in your community.

Some churches grow in number by attracting dissatisfied members of other churches. Such church growth is not true kingdom growth. The members have simply switched seats in the good ship *Hope*. What we need is more people in the ship to heaven, not Christians moving from bow to stern or lower deck to upper deck. Pastors, let's get our churches into a real soul winning program, and leave sheep stealing and sheep baiting to lesser sorts.

Provide everyone with the opportunity to evangelize. A pastor or church should next provide the congregation with as many opportunities to evangelize as possible. We ask individual Christians to handle the altar calls after preparing them for the task. Members also talk to every visitor and stranger in the audience about their souls. (We ask all our visitors to stand so members can identify them for contacts after the service). We also provide a variety of structured situations in which Christians can evangelize, such as park ministries, bus routes, and campus blitzes, among others. In short, we want the average Christian to have the joy of sharing his faith.

The hope of the church lies here. Just as the average communist is active in the propagation of his doctrine, so too church members must spread the gospel. We have a responsibility to expect everyone to evangelize, to equip everyone to evangelize, and to provide the opportunities and motivations to evangelize. If each member led just one soul to Christ each year, the church would easily experience a 50-percent growth. That's with each one winning *just one soul.* If the average Christian can't even do that, then he's not much of a Christian. Pastors, let's make our churches soul-winning churches.

4

Indigenous Principles at Work

For this reason I left you in Crete, that you might set in order what remains, and appoint elders in every city as I directed you *(Titus 1:5)*.

The most important challenge facing the Hispanic church in the last decades of the twentieth century is to become indigenous. By indigenous we mean a church which is self-governing, self-supporting, and self-propagating. The strategy of indigenous church planting has had much success in Latin America and in other portions of the Third World, but the situation north of the Rio Grande is a tragic scene of apathetic Hispanic congregations and ineffective missionary organizations.

Unless the Hispanic churches become indigenous, they will never make a concerted effort to reach the Hispanic world for Christ. Instead they will remain dependent for support and for their very existence on outside sources and will never develop their own outreach ministries.

In this chapter we wish to stress the importance of indigenous church planting. Nonindigenous works are always anemic and apathetic in their functions. They rarely accomplish anything of lasting value in a community and hardly create a ripple in the sea of unbelief. But an indigenous work has the potential of exploding into a dynamic and impressive ministry.

We shall examine the three distinguishing characteristics

of an indigenous work. It is self-governing, self-supporting, and self-propagating.

SELF-GOVERNING

A close fellowship existed among established bodies in the early church (see Acts 20:17; Romans 1:11–12; 1 Corinthians 11:16; Titus 1:5), but the pattern for church organization taught in the New Testament is that of the independent local church. Independent government for the local church has long been practiced in America and Europe with great success. Yet the formation of self-governing works among Hispanics has been slow, painful, and disappointing.

The fault may not be laid entirely to the establishing agencies. Numerous factors affect the Hispanic congregations. Their Roman Catholic background did little to prepare them for an active role in governing the affairs of the church. Converts from Roman Catholicism are shocked to discover that as laity they have a voice in the operation of the church, and they're reluctant to take on the new role.

The totalitarian political climate in Latin American countries has been another hindrance. Hispanics aren't used to having a say in political affairs, and they've learned to distrust political systems. That makes it very difficult for them to function in leadership positions without suspicion or temptations toward autocratic rule. The New England town meetings, which served as the schoolhouse for democracy in North America, never existed south of the border. Consequently Hispanics have little or no experience in self-rule or in reaching a consensus.

The churches also lack proper role models. The average Hispanic church is a poor model of self-rule and discourages the growth of independence in church affairs. And finally, the Anglo church has been rather slow in granting independence or in fostering a spirit of independence in the Hispanic churches they have been led to start.

Trust. It takes trust to establish a self-governing church. The parent church must have confidence in the churches it wishes to establish. A missionary-pastor may be afraid to select men to head the church or to have the church elect its own deacons and elders. He may not think they are spiritually minded to the degree he expects leaders to be. So he hesitates, and in his hesitation real leadership never develops because the men are never given the opportunity.

A mother church may start a separate Hispanic group but never place enough confidence in the group to govern itself. Each attempt by the group to decide its own direction may be seen as a threat to the life of the group or a lack of appreciation for the mother church. Unless the parent church is willing to trust her teenage church, the latter will never grow up to be an adult and produce its own offspring.

Sometimes even Hispanic pastors do not trust their own congregations in self-rule. They run the churches by one-man rule, and when they leave or are taken home, the church collapses for lack of leadership. The Hispanic pastor *must* learn to trust the people he is leading and the men he is working with. If he is to have a core of men to help him lead, he must learn to trust. The intimacy of the brethren, the fact of their conversion through him, and the knowledge of personal sins mitigate against his trust of them, but he must learn objectivity and trust, or the church will never have a core able to govern it.

Train. The next step toward self-rule is the training of the church in self-rule. The church must be taught the idea of self-rule and challenged along those lines.

Begin to set in motion the machinery for self-rule by defining doctrinal positions and explaining the forms of ecclesiastical government, and take the greatest care to delineate the characteristics of good leadership (see 1 Timothy 3:1ff.; Titus 1:5ff.).

Someone has stated that any form of government is good if the leaders are good. We tend to concur with that statement when it comes to church organization. Hence the selection and training of good men is highest on the priority list for self-rule. The congregation can endure almost anything except bad leadership.

The pastor or missionary may select men for these positions (Titus 1:5), or the congregation may be asked to vote for men it feels are worthy of such a position (Acts 6:1ff.). Prior to this selection, men should be encouraged to handle responsible areas of ministry in less official capacities to test their character and train them for future service (1 Timothy 3:10).

The selecting person or body must exercise much patience. Remember that good leaders, like good oak trees, take time to grow. Don't lay hands on men hastily, but dragging your feet may stifle growth (1 Timothy 5:22; 2 Timothy 4:11). A newly wedded husband is not as qualified as his father, yet in his own right he will govern his new home (Ephesians 5:31) and will no doubt grow into his responsibilities (1 Timothy 4:12–16). Measure a man by the standard of the church he is to rule over and not by the standard of the church you come from.

Self-rule will involve risks, but it is essential to the health of the church. As church planters and pastors, we need to remember that the church belongs to Christ and that He is able to guide it even without us, just as He has so wonderfully done for almost two thousand years. We can leave the outcome to Him. Rest on His sovereign grace and rejoice over the privilege to participate in the extension of His church. This is no time to play God or to play dead. Live up to your calling, giving glory to God.

Time. Remember also that self-rule takes time, time to get started and time to perfect.

Getting started is especially hard. The process may appear painfully slow, especially if the group is reluctant to assume the reins of responsibility. The transition from dependence to independence requires the Christian virtue of patience coupled with Solomon's wisdom. It can take as little as six months or as much as six years to transfer authority. Impatience will abort the process, create hostilities, and disperse the rising leadership.

It also takes time to perfect self-rule, if it is possible at all. The young congregation may seem like an organized mess or appear to be on the threshold of civil war. Again, we urge patience. It may take years to develop a good chairman of the deacon board, or a good church moderator. Sometimes abilities lie hidden for a long time, and trust is not gained overnight.

Keep your eye on the flock. The shepherds may not appear to know what they are doing, but they'll bring the flock into the fold by and by. They may not do it exactly your way, but they'll do it just the same.

SELF-SUPPORTING

The second requirement for an indigenous church is that it be self-supporting. A congregation should be able to maintain its own ministry without the financial and material support of other churches or bodies. A group of believers whose pastor is supported by another group is not an indigenous work. A church meeting in a building for which it does not pay rent, and could not pay if expected to, is not an indigenous work. A church which does not buy its own Sunday school materials and other supplies and equipment essential to the existence of its ministries is not an indigenous work.

You may ask, "What is so wrong with this?" The answer is very simple. If a local group cannot maintain its own ministry, how can it ever expand its base of operation? Furthermore, how can it ever be instrumental in starting similar works elsewhere if it cannot help support them in their formative stages? Dependent churches are usually not self-governing, resulting in further weakness.

Expect it. The first step to take in the process of becoming self-supporting is to expect the local group to be self-supporting. The church should be taught to pay its own bills. It should be made to see that the very existence and life of the body depends on the degree to which they are committed. In my experience, little groups take on their own support with great excitement, not with fear or animosity. Presiding over a group of believers which had just received their independence, one believer stood and exhorted the body on the necessity of all sharing financially in the ministry. Others in turn did the same. Ten months later the offerings were exceeding those of the previous months in succession. If we expect it, then they expect it, and if they expect it, then they can do it.

Finances in a church ought to be an open book. If people are expected to govern and support themselves, then they should have the right to decide where their money is to be spent and to know how it *has been* spent. Just as taxation without representation breeds rebellion, so do collection plates without justification or accountability.

Explain the biblical principles. The principles of stewardship and biblical giving need to be adequately explained to every believer and the great passages on giving should be expounded at length (Malachi 3:10; Luke 19:11–27; 1 Corinthians 16:1–2; 2 Corinthians 8–9).

At the same time, nonbelievers should be discouraged from giving. That measure can preserve the church from the charge that it is only after their money and render them much more receptive to a gospel of grace, freely bestowed and freely received (Matthew 10:8). In a Catholic culture, it also helps preserve them from thinking they can do penance.

The Christians should be taught to take care of their pastors and overseers who labor in the Word as their primary occupation and who look to the Lord for their provision. Scriptural passages on this matter need to be taught candidly and unashamedly (1 Corinthians 9:1–14; Galatians 6:6–10;

1 Timothy 5:17–18). When the people of God know fully their responsibility toward their shepherd and when the shepherd throws himself by faith upon their care, the flock responds with great concern for their dear pastor. They would be willing to pluck out their very eyes for him and his family. Hirelings and part-time shepherds can expect no such treatment from God's sheep. If the shepherd lays down his life for the sheep, the sheep willingly give up their fleece to him. He has no need to fleece them.

Other monetary concerns should also be made known to the church. Such concerns as the care of the poor (Acts 6:1ff.), the program of missions (Romans 15:24), the various programs of the church's ministry, even the care of church properties—all these areas become their responsibilities. Congregations should be taught to care for them, not only by their offerings, but also with their physical help.

Expose the church to suffering. Every church needs to learn to pull its own bootstraps. Such "tough love" is essential to independence and indigenous thinking. The new church or small group must be allowed to go through the pains of childbirth. It must suffer a measure of deprivation to learn to depend upon God for all things. As a part of Christ's body a church needs to draw its source from the Head (John 15:4; Colossians 1:18); Christ teaches every part of the body to depend upon Him by faith (Romans 5:1ff.).

A few short years after the church called us to lead them, we embarked upon a major plan to purchase a larger facility to accommodate the expanding church. We sent a letter to every member church of our association soliciting financial assistance in this endeavor. With great anticipation, we awaited the response from God's people. In all, two letters came in response to our solicitation. Only one included money. The pastor expressed his sympathy and his sorrow that he could not include more. In his letter was the vast sum of *one dollar,* and that was all we ever received. I have that dollar on file.

The Lord taught our church, and me especially, the lessons of faith and independence. As a church composed of minorities and lower-middle class Christians, we had been accustomed to the assistance from outside sources. We had not been taught to do it ourselves, even suffering for it. That one dollar received was God's way of saying to us, "You will not get outside help in this area. Whatever you do, you will do on your own. You will learn to be independent from other churches and dependent on Me for all your needs." Since then we have looked to the Lord and to our own members for the financial needs of the church.

The people have learned sacrificial giving. They have learned to give a tithe when they could have a new car. They have given above the tithe, postponing the purchase of their first house, to build the house of God. They have taken days off work to work on the building or to attend special seminars to enrich their Christian lives. In all, we have learned the high price of being an indigenous church: suffering and sacrificing.

The results have been a blessing. Now we can look back at the hand of God in our history. We can honestly say the Lord has brought us this far. God is more real to us as a church than if we had depended upon the gifts and support of other churches. In addition, we have a sense of pride, knowing we had a part in the work of the Lord. A moderately wealthy man (by our standards) stood with me one day as we began a building project and said, "Alex, I would give you all the money for the building now, but the people need to give themselves so they can feel a part of it." He just didn't know how true those words were. As the people gave, they became more of a part of the whole ministry. Now they took pride in "their facility," built with "their money" by "their hands."

The added boon to suffering and succeeding is the confidence it instills in us to attempt greater things. Looking back at what we have done through God's help, we can dream and expect our dreams to become a reality. Now we are looking at an eight-acre site for a new church-school facility. Whether or not we ever get it is not essential. What is essential is the feeling we all have that we could do it if God gives us the opening, something we didn't know a few years ago. The great missionary statesman William Carey said, "Expect great things from God; attempt great things for God!" Only a church that is allowed to suffer at its inception and then grind its way to independent existence can ever attempt big things for God. The Hispanic church needs to let go of the skirts, withdraw its begging palms, roll up its sleeves, and go to work.

Encourage through guarded help. Of course there will be times when the young church will need a little assistance, especially in the early, formative stages. Financial support for the church-planting pastor may be in order with the church eventually assuming all his support. The new church may welcome donations of song books, an old piano, a pulpit, or even the use of a facility. Guarded help lifts morale.

At the moment we are helping two churches, but both are receiving guarded help. We contribute to the partial support of one pastor and give a monthly donation to the other. We help, but we try to make sure they do not depend on us for their existence. The newly formed group sometimes feels as though they can't possibly make it without our help. Yet, we have found they have a new source of energy and faith when they know they have to do it on their own. Help them, but help them more to help themselves.

SELF-PROPAGATING

The next requirement for the indigenous church is that it be self-propagating. It must be expanding through its own efforts, not by the efforts of others.

Teach its importance. Self-propagation is a matter of grave importance. If the church is not taught to reproduce itself, it will not grow. In fact, it will be in great danger of collapsing when the external supports are removed. Time, inertia, and satanic opposition will ensure its demise in one generation. A church that is not self-producing won't even bother to reach its own children, let alone the children of the devil.

Outreach, outreach, outreach is the name of the game. The Great Commission—as well as the great perdition of souls— needs to permeate every fiber of the church. A church must be made to feel that the destiny of the whole world depends on its outreach. When a church is growing, it also plants other churches. We have a very expensive sago palm in our house. Sago palms grow rather slowly, yet from one I have been able to plant two others. In turn I expect these two to produce offspring of their own. In due time I should be able to plant a sago palm in every home in my block. The same principle applies to church growth. Unless a church grows, it will not reproduce and if it doesn't reproduce, a city or nation cannot be gained for Christ.

The whole idea of self-propagation should be prominently present at the inception of the church. It should be part of the infant formula fed the church at birth. Both leaders and members must be taught to propagate their beliefs. The church must act out of belief, not out of obligation. Every church we have helped to plant has been taught to gain its own converts. We don't encourage our members to proselytize from other churches or even visit the sister churches.

Remove the barriers. To help a church become self-propagating, certain barriers must be removed. First is the area of *credibility* or accreditation. A church can be hindered in its growth and outreach by the lack of confidence placed in it by the church planter or mother church. Pastors are kept from preaching or baptizing because they have not been "ordained" or recognized as legitimate pastors by other churches. We do not approve of a-sloppy or standardless ministry, but how can we expect excited men of God to reach out if we are always subjecting them to the approval of someone else? Let them go, but watch them, and you will see more fruit than you've seen in a long time.

Another barrier is *training*. Although training in evangelism may be necessary for soul winning, a soul winner doesn't need training. The story of the two golfers is to the point here. One always had a higher score than the other until the frustrated loser bought his friend a book on golfing and, from that day on, beat him every time. If the church is winning souls, leave it alone. Encourage them to keep on doing what they're doing. If a pastor is successful and growing, leave him alone, don't send him off to a seminary. Now if they are not soul winning, then training and exhortations are a must!

We must remember that some of the greatest moments in church history have been caused not by the intellectual crowd of clergymen, but by the lay preaching of God-ordained men. The same respect must be given the lay preachers God is raising today among Hispanics. A clergyman needs training, but it is more needful that he be filled with the Holy Spirit and God's Word.

Release them. Excitement in religion is a miracle wrought by God and should always be encouraged. The flames of religious excitement need to be fanned and never quenched, directed but never stifled, harnessed for greater effect but never diminished because they appear misdirected. When God's people are moved by the Holy Spirit to evangelize, who are we to hinder them in their zeal? Are we not better advised to imitate the blessed couple who helped Apollos overcome his shallow zeal and so proved the whetstone to this sharp instrument (Acts 18:24–28)?

We have always made it our goal to inspire all Christians to evangelize. The newer the convert, the more "first love" he has and thus the more inspired he is to share that newfound faith. Time will take care of both his zeal and ignorance. Let him alone; guide him if you can, but by no means muzzle his mouth. Albert was such a young convert. Saved from a life of sin, he became quite inspired with the spreading of the gospel. At first Albert was pushy, tactless, and at times embarrassing. The school called once to warn us that a child molester was coming around and talking to little girls, even taking down their names. When the principal described him, it turned out to be our Albert. We didn't tell him to stop witnessing, just to stay off the campus.

Albert grew much in the following months. His zeal made him obnoxious at home, and on several occasions he found himself out on the street with no place to stay. We always urged him to go back home and make up with his folks. Just recently, Albert had the joy of leading his mother to Christ, and he brought her to church. We were all thrilled with him. Albert is still full of zeal, but now he is more directed.

Evangelism can be an explosive affair at times. The whole church may become excited and do the unexpected. Let them. If they are sincere, the gospel is clear, and they are not hurting anyone, why not rather encourage them in this endeavor? Recently we loaded two hundred people in buses and sent them out on door-to-door visitation. The results: a hundred professions of faith and two hundred people filled with the Holy Spirit's power and happiness.

If certain men feel led to start Bible studies and even churches in other parts of the city, don't give them all the reasons why they won't succeed. Let them go. In fact, why not encourage them? A group of five believers came to me to share an idea about starting a church in a certain district. The plan was good, the team was good, so why shouldn't they do it? With my approval they proceeded, and less then twelve months later they are running more than sixty in their services. Did they have a complete course in church planting? No. Did they have positions of church leadership in the present church? No. But they had what it takes: a zeal for lost souls. At times, that's all it takes to build a church.

Recognize the leaders. Churches ought to be organized and recognized as soon as possible. If a little mission church stays a mission too long, it may always be a mission. The point is to reach a group of believers, gather them into a fellowship, organize them into a membership, appoint their leaders, and recognize them as a church. It won't take long for them to attempt to work with the same idea somewhere else and to continue the spontaneous expansion of the Christian church.

Other churches in the fellowship should be guided to recognize their founding pastors as pastors in their own right. Some may not possess the same degree of ministerial training and titles, yet because they are shepherds of flocks and sincere in faith and doctrine, they ought to be duly recognized. Pastor Salazar began to shepherd a small group of Hispanics. Now this church has grown to over 130. He is only twenty-five years old, is not yet ordained, and is in the process of completing his education. Yet to us he is *Pastor* Salazar, a pastor in his own right. We shall do everything to encourage him to build an independent, self-supporting, growing church, and he is doing just that.

My plea to all Hispanics and to those interested in Hispanic works is this: let's go and establish as many independent, self-governing, self-supporting, self-propagating churches as possible. Let's not worry too much about the obstacles. Let's think about the potential!

5

Hispanics in an Anglo Church

There is neither Jew nor Greek, there is neither slave
nor free man, there is neither male nor female; for you
are all one in Christ Jesus (*Galatians 3:28*).

Many Anglo churches have a strong desire to gather in the
harvest of Hispanics pressing all around them. Nowhere is
the love of Christ more evident, the oneness of His church
more visible, and the all-sufficiency of the gospel more
dramatic than in the Anglo desire to evangelize the twenty-
five million Hispanics in America. As an Hispanic pastor and
leader, this radical change is both heartwarming and encouraging, providing for the Hispanic church an inspiration long
overdue.

We believe it is possible for Anglos and Hispanics to be in
the same church, worship the same Lord, and labor together
in His vineyard led by the same Spirit. Many attempts have
been made in times past, some more successful than others.
In this chapter, we wish to share some of the steps an Anglo
church can take to accomplish this dream without it becoming a nightmare. All too easily, Satan can take a good step
and, by his deceitful scheming, use it to further divide the
body of Christ and to hinder the work of evangelism.

One word of caution we offer at this point: make sure your
heart is in it. The pastor himself must be absolutely sold on
the idea. He must first sell his congregation on the dream
and then provide continual encouragement and direction

during the difficult times that follow. If he plans to leave as soon as a foothold is established, he will ruin a good church and abort the success of the mission. Furthermore, the Hispanic believers will look upon him as their pastor. Though he may not know the language and culture, they must sense his commitment to them. The heart is an easier book to read than any other. Also, the Hispanic leadership will turn to him for direction and encouragement and will seek to cooperate with him in the endeavors of the whole church. The pastor *must* be sold on the idea. We cannot emphasize this point enough.

Of course, the ruling boards and members cannot be ignored either. As in any transplant, unless the body is willing to accept the organ, all is lost. Hispanics will appear as a foreign matter to the Anglo body. Unless the body as a whole accepts the new group of members, the effort by the leadership will be futile. Much prayer and preparation must go into the venture. It is important to plan carefully, but always be sensitive to the Holy Spirit's leading as well.

With these introductory words, we shall proceed to lay down guidelines for establishing an Hispanic work in an Anglo church. We shall also warn of pitfalls to avoid along this uncharted course. We beg forbearance here. I can only speak from my limited experience, but I have seen such ministries work.

STEPS TOWARD ESTABLISHING THE WORK

Consider, first of all, the options. Envision the finished product before you begin. Visualize the work and then work the vision. What do you wish to accomplish among Hispanics? Is it just winning them to Christ? Do you simply want to expose them to the Word? Will you leave them alone to be guided by God's Spirit, or will you bring them into your churches? Will you start a Spanish-speaking Sunday school? A church? Or will you worship together in the same pew, shoulder to shoulder? If so, will you use both languages or will you force them to learn English? Or is it possible that you will learn Spanish? Will you have two churches in one building, or will you have a single church? These and other questions must be answered!

The Options

There are a considerable number of options open to you, some of which are, at this point, speculative and idealistic. History, however, and God's sovereignty force us not to close the door on any efforts of evangelism, regardless of how impossible they might seem. Hence if any feel a strong inclination to disregard the recommendations we make, feel assured we are in complete sympathy with any efforts to evangelize the Hispanics and establish them in the most holy faith. Nevertheless, we do feel the following three options are the most reasonable to us, and they are our primary recommendations to the Anglo church.

Separate services. The first and most obvious option is to have two services in the same church, one in English and the other in Spanish. These would meet the individual needs of each group. We have found that Spanish-speaking Hispanics prefer to hear the Word of God in Spanish, and they like to carry on the other aspects of worship, such as prayers, singing, and testimonies, in their native tongue too. Two distinct worship services tailored to the language and cultural needs of the believers is an ideal situation.

This two-service approach gives rise to a question of authority. Is it going to be one church membership in two languages or two church bodies of distinct languages in one church building? The governing board should make a definite decision and should not feel guilty about it.

Under the one-church-two-services approach, one pastor should preside over the whole church, and the governing board should be composed of representatives from both groups with all the members having equal membership.

In the two-services-two-churches approach, two independent Christian assemblies exist in one facility. In actuality, one church is borrowing or renting the church building from another. As long as a harmonious, loving spirit is maintained by both groups, these approaches work equally well. We are indeed hard-pressed to prefer one above the other. When the pastor is bilingual, or at least can communicate with both groups, the one-church-two-services is recommended. If the pastors and the leadership of both groups do not understand each other, the two-churches-two-services is a better choice.

Bilingual services. A second option is the bilingual service. In this approach everyone meets in the same room, regardless of nationality or language. The services are thus translated into the language of the people present. In our case, the English prayers, Bible readings, and sermons, as well as other matters are translated into Spanish. We have seen this done in two ways. If the pastor is bilingual he can translate his own sermon word for word, first giving a sentence or thought in English and then again in Spanish. By interweaving both languages he ministers to both groups. The other way to accomplish a bilingual service is to have one person speak English while a second person stands beside him and translates word for word into Spanish.

The benefits of a bilingual service are evident. The whole body meets together and thus forms itself into a tightly knit group of believers. Of course, it's also more difficult to accomplish. It requires a fluently bilingual preacher or at least people who can help him in the worship services. The services of such people are hard to come by, though we suspect they will be more readily available in the years to come as more Hispanics become bilingual. The other difficulty is that the services are prolonged because almost everything in the service is repeated. Long services, though acceptable to Hispanics, are not delightful to the average Anglo congregation. Like anything else, however, believers can learn patience with one another and make this work.

One English service. A third option is for the Anglo church to insist on one English-speaking ministry, and thus force all Hispanics to accommodate themselves to the English language and customs. We do not consider this entirely bad. There are sections in America where the majority of the Hispanics are predominantly English-speaking and would have little or no difficulty relating to and understanding the worship services in English. Indeed, a good many of the Anglo churches have a smattering of Hispanics in their churches and on the roll books, though they may not be aware of it. These Hispanics have blended in so well to the Anglo lifestyle that they are difficult to isolate and classify as a minority group.

Unfortunately this group is small. Furthermore, the rise of nationalism and cultural pluralism have put pressure on even this Hispanic segment to identify with their own group. So unless the Anglo church makes a concentrated effort to reach English-speaking Hispanics, they will not join, even though they know the language and the culture. Blindness to this fact can be devastating to both groups.

What then can be done by the Anglo church to attract the English-speaking Hispanic to an English-speaking service and church? The question calls for much imaginative thinking. Here are some recommendations:

1. Give the few Hispanic believers in the church high visibility. For example, let them usher, lead singing, do Bible readings, or play special musical numbers.
2. Invite gifted and qualified Hispanic preachers to share the pulpit without calling the service an Hispanic service. Make it a routine service with a special speaker.
3. Have the preachers and teachers make cultural comments, not puns, jokes, or defamatory remarks. For instance, if you say, "When you sit down to have your steak and eggs . . ." also add, ". . .and when you sit down to have your tacos and rice and beans." This strikes home to English-speaking Hispanics.

4. Play up Hispanic individuals as illustrations without appearing to be condescending to the Hispanic population.

These are some suggestions. You will have to come up with others. The key is to make the Hispanic feel at home without making the Anglo uncomfortable. If you can do this, more power to you.

The obvious drawback in this approach is the omission of all the Spanish-speaking Hispanics. If there should be—as unlikely as it seems—no Spanish-speaking segment present, then proceed with haste to reach out to the Hispanics that are around you.

This third option is neither the favorite nor the most fruitful in terms of numbers. Anglo churches immersed in Hispanic communities should accommodate the needs of the Spanish-speaking to worship God in their own tongue. This is a more reasonable, fruitful, and equitable approach, and God will bless its use.

The Steps

As in all evangelistic efforts and church-planting endeavors, what works for you may not work in exactly the same way for another. Hence the steps we outline in the following paragraphs are suggestive of what your church may pursue in the effort to form an Hispanic group. Our strategy has four elements: leadership, evangelism, acceptance, and development.

Leadership. Probably the first major step the Anglo church should take is to select the proper leadership for the program. The success of the work depends as much on the person or persons leading it as on goals that have been set. The program needs the right captain to guide it safely through the treacherous reefs that have sunk so many previous efforts. The burden of reaching the Hispanic is not new. Others have carried it close to their hearts, but often they failed to realize their dreams because they lacked the proper personnel.

Select a man of Hispanic thinking—one sympathetic to the needs of the Hispanics and loyal to the Anglo-Christian community. A woman will not do, because of cultural and biblical standards (1 Corinthians 14:34). He must be qualified as a leader (not a novice or unstable Christian), with sound character, a zeal for Christ, and a great love for people. It is more important that he be a winner of souls than a theological giant. Formal theological training is not essential. Whichever option the church uses, such a man must be able to communicate to the church's leadership. He need not be fluent in English if he is to preach in Spanish, but he must be submissive to the pastor and principles of the Anglo church to insure the success and harmony of the Hispanic group. In addition, all that we have said elsewhere about Hispanic pastors applies here.

Evangelism. The goal must be to evangelize. Efforts at evangelizing the Hispanic have failed because of a half-hearted apologetic effort. The same zeal and vehemence found in Moody, Sunday, and Finney must be directed toward Hispanics without fear of turning them off. The goal must be to bring individual Hispanic men and women face to face with the Person and claims of Jesus Christ. They need to be saved just like any other human being, and the same methods used to save others may be of use in winning them to Christ.

No means must be spared in bringing Hispanics to their knees before Christ. A Spanish-speaking Sunday school class can be of great value both in providing a central place for other Christians to invite their Spanish-speaking friends, as well as a place of evangelism and Bible teaching. Bible classes in the homes of new Christians have been very profitable among Hispanics. Special Spanish-speaking services in the church, when well-publicized and coordinated, have also proven useful. When all else has been tried, turn to door-to-door or home visitation. The best is to try all of them and to persevere in these methods, regardless of how meager the results might be.

Keep in mind that the Hispanic church will not grow if the individual Hispanics are not regenerated through the saving grace of Christ. Social programs, charity efforts, and intercultural exchanges, while good, work against church growth in the long run if they are not a means by which to proclaim the gospel of Christ. Sure, the Hispanics need mercy, but they also need to be born again. Let's never forget that.

Acceptance. A third step in this endeavor is the acceptance of the new Hispanic believers by the Anglo church. I visited a large Anglo church recently and was shocked to see how few people actually bothered to greet me. In all, less than six people actually spoke to me, though many more looked at me as though I were a foreigner. If I, a pastor, felt uncomfortable, imagine how another Hispanic visitor would feel. By contrast, when I was a young field hand in a small town in central California, a few of us attended an all-white Baptist church. You can imagine four brown faces in a sea of white. But this church made special arrangements to have us accepted. They even invited the four of us to a special dinner of moose meat, and we were the only guests present. We wanted to go back to that church.

Unless the pastor, the leadership, and the body as a whole go out of their way to make the Hispanics feel accepted, they will undoubtedly not attend again. Welcoming committees need to be established. Individual Christians should show them around, sit with them in church, and introduce them to other friends. Young peoples' groups should be alerted to this display of love.

The new Hispanic Christian is doubly sensitive. First, he is a new Christian in a setting foreign to his accustomed way of worshiping. Second, he is conscious of standing out as an Hispanic among "gringos." A careless word or gesture may be enough to turn him off. If he does not feel accepted, he will not return. Nor will he invite others to join him. And the church will miss its chance to create a sizable Hispanic group of believers.

Development. Once you have won a nucleus of Hispanics to Christ and have adopted that nucleus into the church family, you're ready to begin the process of developing it into a church—or into an organized branch of the overall church. Start a membership list and encourage a group identity. You must identify, select, and train leadership, plan social activities, and organize evangelistic efforts. In all, the church must be both encouraged to grow spiritually and motivated to reach out to others. The sooner the Hispanics learn to run "their own shop," the sooner growth will take place. Finally, the same biblical principles for church organization that apply to Anglo churches should apply to Hispanics.

The Pitfalls

The Anglo church has made a mess of incorporating Hispanics into their churches. Here and there we see a candle burning brightly, but these are exceptional. We would like to list some of the pitfalls which lie in your way. Avoid them at all cost if you are serious about this matter.

Prejudice. Bigotry lurks in all of our hearts and needs only a drop of venom to show its ugly head. Hispanics can point to a trail of bloodshed running through their history because of prejudice. They may accept your God based upon the infallible Word of God, but accepting your fellowship is a different matter, for such is based upon the human heart, and many a heart has a history of racial prejudice. Be sure of the choice. Some Anglos will leave because of Hispanic associations. Once your lot is cast, don't change your mind. A church that rethinks its Hispanic outreach because of negative vibrations from a few bigots will show its true colors to the whole Hispanic community and will lose them all.

Imbalanced programs. The larger group will tend to monopolize everything. Special consideration should be made for the smaller group. It is easy for the ruling board to enact programs designed to meet the needs of the Anglo community and unintentionally disregard those of the Hispanic. Everything from special services to social activities may be designed in such a way that the Hispanic group becomes mere spectators. In one of our New Year's services we committed such an act by planning all our activities in English and unintentionally omitted from participation the Spanish-speaking element in the body. Regardless of the imbalance in numbers, there needs to be a balance in meeting the needs of each group.

Intimidation. Up to now, Hispanics in North America have displayed a timid, unassuming role. Things will probably change in the future. Yet as long as the Anglo community holds a superiority in numbers, wealth, and expertise and as long as a good part of the Hispanic population are refugees or recent immigrants, there is going to exist a feeling of inferiority on the part of many Hispanics.

The Anglo leadership must be careful not to intimidate the Hispanic church or its leadership. Just how is this done? Intimidation may show up in the use of language, money, knowledge, or sheer pressure from the ruling body. Preaching against illegal aliens and the like has a negative effect. Talking philosophy or strategy with Hispanic pastors or lay leaders in university terms only makes them feel more inadequate and discourages cooperation. Excellency in Anglo programs should be used to inspire, not impress. You can have high-society meetings and mannerisms, but don't impose them on Hispanics. Speaking of Hispanics as "uncultured," "backward," "low class," "ignorant," or "unsophisticated" does not help.

Acculturation. The Anglo church needs to be careful about a process called "acculturation." By this we mean the loss of the Hispanic identity and the assimilation of the Hispanic into the Anglo mold. True, we must all become Americans. Yet some Hispanics so lose their identity that they disdain being referred to as Hispanic and refuse to work among Hispanics. Our large Anglo Bible colleges and seminaries can work against the Hispanic community by unwittingly turning out an Anglo minister in a brown body.

I had a chance recently to speak about this to a group of foreign students at a large Bible college on the West Coast. My title was "Go Home," for the same thing happens to foreign students in America. They pick up the ways of Anglo America and soon lose their ability to relate to their own people. Still others love the delicacies and luxuries of America and prefer not to go back to the poverty of their own countries. Some do it out of fear, others from pride, and still others from greed.

The way to stem the tide of assimilation is by placing the Hispanic in a ministry to Hispanics. Still another way is by helping the Hispanic to be proud of his or her heritage. Again, they can be encouraged to think of the needs of their people and the key ways they can be of help to them.

Dependence. It will be natural for the Hispanic church or group to become dependent upon the Anglo church for everything—for money, ideas, buildings, leadership, and even encouragement. Once an Hispanic church or group becomes *parasitic,* the effort at growth is stifled and the Anglo church is host to a group which neither contributes to the ministry nor exemplifies a live Hispanic outreach.

The Hispanic group or church must be taught to shoulder its share of the responsibilities of operating a church. They must be taught to support their pastor, clean and maintain their building, provide means for growth, and cooperate with other existing church bodies. The more independent and self-sufficient the group becomes, the easier the burden on the Anglo church and the more other Anglo churches are tempted to imitate the pattern.

Paternalism. Akin to dependence is Anglo paternalism. Some Anglo churches never intend for the Hispanic church or group to have a sense of independence. An Hispanic pastor met with an Anglo pastor to discuss the starting of an Hispanic work in the church. The Anglo body was about to build a new sanctuary and let the Hispanic group use the old one. The Hispanic said, "Don't be surprised if the Hispanic group grows larger than the Anglo group and forces them back into the smaller sanctuary."

The Anglo pastor replied, "Then we will do just that." That's the right spirit to succeed in Hispanic work.

Segregation. Out of the dark ages comes a form of segregation that is "Ichabod" to Hispanic-Anglo relations. Some churches believe "races" should be kept segregated, and no manner of fellowship encouraged. So-called inter-marriages—and, obviously, interracial dating—are discouraged. The Christian church must deal with this smear and defamation of the true body of Christ. Root this sin out, or it will root out the Hispanic element in your church.

Expectations. Be patient with the Hispanic church. If the Anglo expectations are too high, the Hispanic church will miscarry or fly away to more understanding parents. They will never do things as well as you do them—not for at least a decade. The Anglo church has had two hundred years to perfect its doctrine, organization, and programs. We cannot expect a fledgling group to meet it at full run. Be patient, understanding, and supportive. They will come of age. They will not be exactly like you. You wouldn't want that. But they will be a group you will be proud of.

We trust these few insights will be of benefit to our Anglo churches. Hispanics can and should be reached. The Anglo church, or any other ethnic church, can reach out to Hispanics to fulfill the great commission. All they need is a little help. Why not take up this challenge and give it a chance in your church? You'll be glad you did.

6

Organization and Administration

I am writing these things to you, hoping to come to you before long; but in case I am delayed, I write so that you may know how one ought to conduct himself in the household of God, which is the church of the living God, the pillar and support of the truth (1 Timothy 3:14–15).

I need to say a word about the organization and administration of Hispanic churches. I will approach the issue through Hispanic eyes for Hispanics, hoping to lay out information and insights suitable for work among Hispanics.

For a ministry to be successful, it must be organized and administered properly. Yet I must confess that in my own ministry I have found this to be the area of greatest challenge.

Highly organized cultures and societies like those in Europe and North America need little advice on organization. But Third World nations generally lack the sophistication and organizational skills of the modern nations. For many, the lack of organization is the noose around their necks threatening their very survival. That is certainly the case in church organization and management.

Few Hispanic churches have more than two hundred members. Among other reasons for this smallness is the lack of skills in the formation and operation of a large church. A powerful preacher may fill the building, but only an astute organizer and administrator can build the large crowd into an organized church capable of sustained growth. Basic courses in management and administration are either lacking or deficient in preparing the average Hispanic pastor for this challenge ahead of him.

Perhaps the hints and suggestions in this chapter can help those trying to be good administrators and challenge us all to work harder at it.

KEYS TO EFFECTIVE ORGANIZATION

"A house divided against itself cannot stand." These were the wise words of our Lord (Matthew 12:25). The purpose of organization is to keep the whole from falling apart through individualism or lack of corporate direction. Organization serves a dual purpose: to hold everything together and to keep everyone going in the same direction. How many churches do you know that have broken up because of faulty organization? Let us explore some keys to effective organization which are essential in Hispanic ministries.

Scriptural soundness. The first and foremost word on church organization is that it must be scripturally sound. Hispanics are in a state of upheaval, doubting much, if not all, of their religious heritage. Rejecting a system based on medieval principles and superstitious beliefs, they are brought, through the preaching of the Word, to place their utmost confidence in the Holy Book. It becomes, and rightfully so, the only basis for faith and practice. Our motto is "We believe the Bible, the whole Bible, and nothing but the Bible."

Our churches must be established upon principles laid down in Scripture if they are to endure the constant and increasing scrutiny of the emerging church. Growing believers, taught to honor the Word, will question the validity of their churches if they are founded on principles other than what is clearly spelled out in the Word of God.

The problem of church splits over doctrinal issues can be prevented by a clear understanding of what the church stands for. One of our first moves in the church was to establish a church constitution which would serve a useful purpose. A church constitution is a tool which can be of great benefit to the church in the long run. It should contain the clear doctrinal position of the body so it can prevent movements in the membership against the established order. The divisive issues of salvation by grace or works, the issue of tongues, the doctrines of angels, hell, heaven, even the position of the Word of God, and the Person of Christ can be covered in the constitution.

Since our church does not hold to the practice of speaking in tongues, we do not admit anyone to membership who cannot subscribe to our constitution. By that we avoid the problem of either contending with the person or of reviewing the matter every time it comes up. We just don't hold to it, so there is no need to discuss it or argue about it. Hence, it never becomes a church issue, and we will never have a church split over it. I mention this not to argue the merits of speaking in tongues, but only to illustrate how a clearly defined statement of faith can prevent problems over doctrinal issues. A constitution serves the church well in matters like this. In fact, any policy critical to the church's ministry can be spelled out clearly in the constitution. Of course, in certain states a constitution is also a requirement for permission to operate as a tax-exempt, nonprofit organization.

But we must emphasize that only what is scriptural should go into a church constitution. Matters contrary to the Word of God, however expedient they may seem, should have no part in a church constitution! A word to the wise is sufficient.

Simplicity. The second most important aspect of organization to be kept in mind is simplicity in organization. The difficulty with adopting ready-made organizational structures or patterns from existing North American institutions is their complexity. The average Latin American mind is not accustomed to the large, complex machinery needed to operate the average North American church. The more complex the system, the more danger there is for the church to fragment or to lose its direction.

Some organization patterns in American churches call for numerous boards with a seemingly endless list of committees and subcommittees. In many, an administrator is hired to handle this octopus-like creation. For minds accustomed to such operations it becomes a routine matter. But most Hispanics do not live in complex spheres. In time, more and more of them will step into the computer rooms and large administrative offices of giant corporations and banking institutions. Until that day arrives, simplicity must be the word.

What do we mean by simplicity? We mean the easiest and least complicated way to get the job done. Church boards have an unusual way of making complex a perfectly simple situation. Someone has said that the camel is a horse put together by a committee. The pastor must work hard at keeping things as simple as possible.

Keep church programs as simple as possible. Programs should not overlap or duplicate themselves. Find the programs which pay off and stick to them. We have built our ministry on five basic programs.

The Sunday morning preaching service is the main breadwinner for the church. There we concentrate on evangelism, dissemination of information, collection of tithes, welcoming of new visitors, and giving publicity to the Word of God and the ministry of the church. It is *the* church service, and everything else revolves around it. More time and money is spent on it than any other service, though we also have a Sunday evening inspirational service.

The next program on the list is WIN, our evangelism program. It is held on Tuesday evenings all year round. No other program or church activity is planned on this evening. People are encouraged to attend. It has a paid director and a special budget. The purpose of the program is to train soul winners and to win people to Christ. It provides an army of preachers and thus keeps a never-ending supply of soul winners on the front lines causing the church to grow. Without this program, the church would lose much of its drive to grow and to reach out to people. Here is the heartbeat for growth and for missions.

The third program is the Sunday school held on Sunday morning. There the whole church is divided according to age and marital status. Each group receives its own instruction according to its needs. All high schoolers meet in one room, all the junior highers in another, single parents in another, and so on. The planning of social activities for all age groups is also done in the Sunday school, thus meeting the spiritual and social needs of everyone in the church. Properly balanced, the Sunday school is a wonderful discipleship tool ministering to the total person.

The fourth program is the Wednesday evening Family Night, which consists of a special program of inspiration and instruction for adults and a concurrent program of activities and instruction for the children. Intensive Bible study is provided along with a great deal of congregational singing. The whole family is invited and planned for. The children are given prime consideration with wholesome, supervised games and activities, along with in-depth instruction. For many, it is a midweek shot-in-the-arm to keep them going until Sunday. This is the third-best-attended program, next to the Sunday morning service and Sunday school.

The fifth thrust is the Friday film ministry. This is a many-faceted program consisting of films, musical programs, and prayer meetings, all held on Friday evening. The program serves to bring the family together for a wholesome time of inspiration and fellowship. Effective use is made of gospel films for outreach. It pays off by winning souls and exposing the church to many who would not come to a church service. It also gives Christians one more opportunity during the week to meet for encouragement. For new believers it is essential for survival.

In all of these major programs, we provide good care: baby sitting, parking attendants, ushers and hostesses, and the best music. We also use a public address system, and record sermons for future use and sale.

Many other activities take place during the week, including baseball games, men's and women's meetings, home Bible studies, and special prayer meetings, but all of them take second place to the five major programs of the church, which have a prior claim on the church's resources and schedule. When someone has an idea for a new program, that person may pursue it as long as it doesn't compete with the existing five programs. No baseball league could ever play on Tuesday evening. No series of home Bible studies could get started on Wednesday night. No social group can be organized outside the Sunday school. Hence, we have a simple and workable overall program.

The church then has the luxury of concentrating on a few good programs. It does not wear out the faithful few with a whole lot of whirlwind activities that do not produce the desired results or that compete with similar programs. The pastor can concentrate on handling the five irons in the fire and doesn't have to fret himself with every novel idea suggested to him by the board or parishioners.

I would recommend to any pastor that he find three or four good programs designed to meet the needs of the church (Acts 2:42) and concentrate his energies on making a go of them. Design programs around these ideas. Then work the programs. Always work on improving existing programs first before attempting to start new programs. A program that works should never be discarded over one which has never been tried. "A bird in the hand is worth two in the bush." In essence, keep it simple.

Social acceptance. The organization of the church should be socially acceptable to the people. Certain things are rather hard for Hispanics to accept as part of church organization. The Salvation Army will always have difficulty winning great acceptance because of the perceived contradiction of a pastor in a soldier's uniform. Under General Booth it may have worked, but not under sensitive Hispanics accustomed to meekness in their spiritual leaders.

The place of women in leadership is another anathema. Now it is true that some churches have women as pastors and lay leaders, but such churches are small and not very strong. Hispanic men have a great disdain for women telling them what to do. Weak men will sit under a woman's leadership, but strong men—never. So why complicate the church's function by a socially unacceptable organizational pattern? (Personally I believe the Scriptures also provide a basis for men leading the church: 1 Timothy 2:9–15; 3:1–8.) A church will do well to place men in positions of leadership and let the women minister to the women and children (Titus 2:3–5).

Robert's Rules do well in England and America, but not too many Hispanics are acquainted with dear *Roberto*. If they must be used, then explain them properly and educate the whole congregation in the use of this organizational procedure. It works well, once you get used to it, but it may also be a headache. A good system of checks and balances is always good, and praise God for prayer.

Let me ask you this: how do you translate First Southern Baptist Church into Spanish? I say, don't. In my community I came across an Hispanic church bearing that name, but in Spanish. Bewildered, I stood in front of the church trying to figure out how a southern church happened to be in East Los Angeles. Then it dawned on me! This was a Southern Baptist Church (in Spanish it doesn't make sense). Why not give the church a name that identifies the people, not the denomination? You'll have greater success.

Mi general! ("My general!") Although Hispanic society is changing in many aspects, there still prevails a strong sense of *caudillismo*, involving male—and even one-man—leadership. In Hispanic society this tends to verge on a benevolent dictatorship. It proves to be both a curse and a blessing, depending on the character of the man in charge. But the pattern may be put to good use by church planters and pastors of growing infant churches. I believe a firm hand at the outset, when other *caudillos* are vying for authority in the church, is critical to the survival of the fledgling congregation. We underestimate both the devil and the sinister motives of men if we think this problem will not arise (see 3 John 9). I speak from experience.

As the body matures, as trust and loyalty develop, and as men learn how to work together, the gradual shift to plurality of leadership may be safely undertaken. Respectable and sincere men can make decisions together on major issues. The church will always need a strong leader, but not necessarily in the *caudillo* mold of days gone by.

Styles. A fourth key to effective organization is the style adopted by both church and pastor. At first the pastor forms the style of the church, but in time a larger church will dictate the style of the preacher who ministers to it. We could say much about the forms of administration, but here I want to emphasize the overall style of the church.

The church should be styled around expression. Hispanics are an emotional bunch and lend themselves easily to expression. Cold, expressionless worship services accompanied by stiff, stagnant preaching do little to attract the hearts of Hispanics. This is one of the main reasons the Pentecostal churches have made such gains among them. In a typical Pentecostal service, worshipers clap their hands to the music as they sing their hymns, often to the accompaniment of tambourines. "Hallelujahs" and "amens" make up nearly half the sermon, and they come from the audience, not the preacher. Any church ministering to Hispanics must provide worshipers an avenue of expression. We permit guitars in our services, play the piano with a lively beat, clap our hands to certain choruses (*coritos*), and encourage the people to respond to the preacher with "amens."

Hispanics love to sing! A good song leader is vital to a worship or evangelistic service. The best way to thin a crowd is to have a dead or expressionless song service. I believe that the organ, unless played with a certain excitement, is best fit for funerals and the like. Lively, meaningful songs should be selected. Songs should speak to the heart, not just the head. Guitars are *the* instruments of the Hispanics. How dare we keep them out of the religious life of the people! With guitars, the Latin man wins the heart of his beloved. Why not permit him to sing to his new Beloved!

By style we also mean a church built on warm and personal fellowship. The influence of Roman Catholicism is waning because it fails to meet the Hispanic's greatest social need, the need for social acceptance. Poverty has driven the Hispanic family to seek its joy in itself. The result is a tightly knit extended family that thrives on the times spent socializing. The weekly visit before the cold altar of a Roman Catholic church, the expressionless preaching and mass, and the quick exodus of mute worshipers leaves the soul craving for more. That "more" is the feeling of warmth found when a church is more than a classroom to teach dogma, a place to meet with people we love.

We insist on fellowship. Our deacons are instructed to keep the doors of the church open at least one hour after the service. On a typical Sunday, the people will not go home immediately after the service but will linger in the halls and patios until well over two hours after the preacher has gone out of the pulpit. Others make arrangements to meet in local coffee shops or at homes to continue their time of fellowship. A preacher who thinks his people should go home after the service so he can get home too is shortchanging his people and himself. He will breed a type of Protestant mass with all its accompanying evils and will find his church the poorer because of it. The costs incurred in time and utility bills are easily defrayed by a loving, fulfilled congregation. Pastors and church leaders need to give the people time and space to love one another at their leisure.

Another aspect of style which I believe is essential is what I call "ecclesiastical looseness." Hispanics are not an uptight people. In fact, they may even seem lazy and irresponsible to many Anglos. It's true that the workaholic among Hispanics is as rare as the dodo bird, but they are not, as a group, lazy. They are just much looser about life. Agrarian and rural in habit, they have taken on the demands of the environment. By contrast, a highly industrialized America produces a society which, from the Hispanic point of view, is uptight, cold, impersonal, and at times, rude.

Hispanics are habitually late, so forget about trying to start everything right "on time." There is American standard time, and there is Mexican standard time. The latter runs around fifteen minutes behind the former. Not even brides show up at their weddings on time. (I know one who was two hours late!) Anglos will never understand this phenomenon, but among Latins it is a fact of life. When I first came to the pastorate of First Fundamental Bible Church, the evening service began at 7:30, although it was scheduled for 7:00. Mind you, 7:30 was when the person in charge showed up! Little by little, we have weaned the people from tardiness and now we usually start at 7:05.

"Looseness" also keeps the Hispanic from being highly organized. Great, involved, exotic plans are doomed to fail; they are just too elaborate and complicated. "This one thing I do" is our motto. Few of us are geared up to do more than one thing at a time. I recall meeting with a representative from a Christian group that focused on college campus ministry. He outlined for me a complicated but complete program of evangelism and discipleship for the local church. As he explained it, I kept thinking, our people won't even understand this, let alone carry it out. Not a single Hispanic church ever used it. How could they? It was designed for North American college students, not the Hispanic mind. Now, it's not that Hispanics are incapable of comprehending such intricate programs; it's just not their way of doing things.

Our soul-winning program is a slight variation on the "Evangelism Explosion" method of Dr. James Kennedy. His method is excellent, one of the finest soul-winning training programs around. Our only problem with it was its complicated format. I condensed it and simplified the language, and we have used it successfully for over ten years. Again the whole idea was to keep only one thing at a time before the people. Not accustomed to dealing with many issues at one time, they would not respond favorably to any program which would burden them. This kind of looseness must always be kept in mind. Of course, too much looseness becomes a purposeless, disorganized mess.

KEYS TO EFFECTIVE ADMINISTRATION

I wish to focus my attention now on the administration of the local church, and in particular, the Hispanic church. Administration is not my gift, a weakness I confess most candidly. Yet I feel it is necessary to say a few things about it—especially since the majority of my fellow ministers may have the same weakness.

Clear philosophy of ministry. At the top of our administrative task is the formation of a clearly defined philosophy of ministry. I have taken mine from Colossians 1:28: "And we proclaim Him, admonishing every man and teaching every man with all wisdom, that we may present every man complete in Christ." Translated into a workable plan, it means preaching the gospel to every soul so they can be born again, and then taking that new babe in Christ and teaching him all there is to know of Christ until we can present each person complete in Christ at His coming or at the person's death. The whole plan involves the twofold ministry of evangelism and edification. One does not supercede the other. Each must receive the utmost care and diligence.

The establishment of a clear philosophy of ministry will keep us from changing directions in the middle of the stream. It will also prevent us from altering our course when the winds of change blow hard against the ship. Hispanic churches are always on the verge of becoming sidetracked on social and political issues. They are also subject to infection by the wandering maverick churches and religious movements out of Anglo Protestantism and to the tireless efforts of Catholics to woo these "separated brethren" back into the fold. In short, establish a philosophy of ministry and build the church on it. And do not discard it after a few years of success or even of failure.

Consistent style of leadership. The second key to effective administration is for the pastor and church to have a consistent style of leadership. Differing styles are required for the various stages of development in the church. The personality of the individual pastor will naturally gravitate towards a particular style of leadership.

At the early stage of development, the Hispanic church *probably* needs a more autocratic style of leadership. By autocratic I don't mean a dictator, but a pastor who can provide strong, decisive leadership. As the church develops, the style of leadership may change to a more nondirectional, group-decision-making style. The question of plurality in leadership need not be discussed here. To form a strong church one does not need to have plurality of leadership, but the pastor or church planter must know what he is doing from the start. Experience is helpful. Courage and humility must be well-mixed! Above all, he must possess a great deal of sanctified common sense.

I recommend a strong pastoral leadership for two reasons. One is the inexperience of the church members, especially lay leaders. Most of the men in lay leadership positions have no experience in the decision-making process of church government and they don't really understand enough of Scripture to make confident judgments. They need someone to give them strong direction. Anglo churches differ here because of their long tradition and because, in many instances, the leadership is composed of laymen with seminary education or at least some sophisticated theological instruction.

The second reason for this recommendation lies in the root of the Hispanic culture (although it may actually come from our sinful nature). The prevalence of *personalismo* or *caudillismo*, the individualistic attitude of our men, makes a young church very susceptible to church splits. Plurality of leadership among a group of men who have not learned submission or cooperation only exposes the church to the danger of breaking up into factions. The danger is all too real to pass by. Experience has taught me to be on guard for it all the time, especially from traveling Bible teachers or ex-pastors. They may be wolves in sheep's clothing seeking to gather a flock for themselves at someone else's expense (see Acts 20:28–31; Romans 16:17–18).

The danger of a strong, autocratic pastoral style of leadership is the inability of the leader to grow with the church. In essence, the church will grow only as large as the style of leadership will allow it to grow. The pastor *must* train his lay leaders to submit, to work together, and to be loyal to one another. A pastor who wants to build a large work must devote some serious study to styles of leadership and to the training of lay leaders. Otherwise, unless he is especially gifted, he will be doomed to frustration and discouragement.

Competent staff. No pastor can do the work all by himself. Sooner or later he must solicit the assistance of others. He will need to gather a pastoral staff around him to help him execute the office of church leader. Who and how many will be dictated both by the size of the church budget and the size of the membership. As every church leader knows, delegation of duties is imperative to personal survival. Jethro gave Moses this advice and warned him by saying, "You will surely wear out, both yourself and these people who are with you, for the task is too heavy for you; you cannot do it alone" (Exodus 18:18).

The first staff member a pastor should have is a competent church secretary who can arrange the details of the church office, intercept phone calls, screen visitors, arrange visits, and help disseminate information to the other members of the church. She gives the church an open-for-business look and greatly aids in the preservation of the pastor's energy and time. The secretary should be followed by a visitation minister to help run the evangelism program of the church. He should also be available to do personal, home, office, and hospital visits for the sake of soul winning. A good evangelist will raise his support in two or three months by the number of souls he wins to Christ. The evangelist need not be a pulpiteer. His strengths should lie in personal work.

Other staff members to add are a Christian education director to run the Sunday school and other programs, a youth director, and a music minister. Hispanic churches should also make every effort to put a competent marriage counselor on staff in addition to these others—or before them if the pastor is not strong on counseling.

Cautions. We would like to close this section on organization and administration with several words of warning to church leaders. A man can be a gifted preacher with a pastor's heart, but if he lacks some basic administrative skills, he will fail as an effective pastor.

Beware of *sloth.* Administration is hard—not always desirable—work. Sermon preparation, preaching, counseling, and soul winning are far more enjoyable than the task of administration. Yet it must be done.

Remember to *stroke* your people. Our people will work for us if we tell them we appreciate them. Find out what motivates people and then do those things. Too often we complain of people not wanting to work. My experience is that they want to work. We just don't show them appreciation. We don't stroke them enough.

Don't be too soft. Effective administration calls for firm decisions. Incompetent staff must be rebuked or chastized, or even dismissed. Church leaders must be kept in line. We must be compassionate, but not softees. We must be meek, but not weak, *mansos pero no mensos* ("meek, but not stupid").

Be *sincere*. Leaders must not be manipulative. It is very easy to administer with a deep sense of sincerity and honesty. Our people must know that programs exist for the people and not people for the programs. Running over people to get a job done is not only poor administration, it's also wrong. Their welfare is more important than our ambitions and goals. Sometimes we will have to apologize for ineffective planning or programming. We should not be ashamed to do so.

Don't be a simpleton. Study the whole business of administration. Just as no modern corporation can survive with incompetence at the administrative level, neither will our churches survive. A minister should take courses in and read books on church administration. As the church grows, so must our skills. It takes more skill to run the local Safeway supermarket than the mom-and-pop store in the *barrio*. The same analogy applies to church ministries.

In this chapter I have given some information on organization and administration. Much has been written on the subject but not much with Hispanics in mind. May these few lines help some minister do a great work for God in the *barrio*. It can be done. I know. I've seen it happen!

7

Hispanic Men and Women

There is neither Jew nor Greek, there is neither slave nor free man, there is neither male nor female; for you are all one in Christ Jesus (*Galatians 3:28*).

In composing this volume on the Hispanic, it's not always easy to know what to include or exclude, but a discussion on the peculiarities of men and women would definitely be in order. Here we shall endeavor to list some unique characteristics of Hispanic men and women in hopes of making it easier to minister to them and with them.

HISPANIC MEN

Our men are famous for the *macho* mystique, the he-man image. Part true and part false, *machismo* does permeate our culture, but not always in the stereotypical way popularized in films, television, and other forms of the mass media.

Men and Their Importance in Society

The man dominates the Hispanic culture. First of all, he rules the home. At least he likes to think he does, and his wife wants him to feel he does. The Hispanic male is also the kingpin in society. Public office is a man's world. In fact, the prevailing view is that if a man does not do it, then it must not be too important. Every organization in the Hispanic community—the church included—must take this attitude seriously.

Our churches have suffered much because of the wrong view the church has had of its men, and the terrible picture the church has given to the world. As a non-Christian, I saw the Christian church as a female-dominated society in which a real man didn't belong.

The Characteristics of Hispanic Men

The Hispanic male is in most respects identical to the males of most other cultures, including his Anglo counterpart. However, there are a few peculiar characteristics worth noting.

1. Dominant. The Hispanic male is dominant, sometimes to an extreme. He will not take a second seat to a woman, especially his wife. Whenever you find an Hispanic man doing that, he is most likely henpecked or alienated from the cause his wife espouses. Anglo missionaries or Christian workers may take a woman's zeal as evidence of her dedication and figure her husband will come right along. They are surprised when he doesn't and when he actually stands aloof. In fact, the more attention given to this boisterous woman, the farther removed the man becomes. Why? Because he is the boss and will not subject himself to any place or anyone who elevates his wife above him.

When Anglo workers give Hispanic women responsibilities normally reserved for men just because they have more time or seem to be "more spiritual," they are driving a wedge between the church and the mainstream of the Hispanic community. Caution must be taken with this phenomenon. The male is dominant, and nothing we say will change that.

2. Define manliness differently. Hispanic males define their manliness in a way much different from their Anglo brethren. Reread the first chapter of this volume to refresh your mind. Hispanic males respect strength, age, maturity, ability to communicate, and personal magnetism. Courage is given a high priority. Money, good looks, and education are not as important to the Hispanic male.

3. Defer child rearing to the wife. The woman's place is in the home. The traditional Hispanic still thinks this is true. He delegates the task of raising children to his wife. Her place is with the kids. That's why the children are usually more attached to the mother than to him. He loathes changing diapers, baby-sitting, washing clothes, or for that matter, any job associated with child rearing. Much of this is cultural insensitivity to the needs of his family. However, much of it is also biblical. We must know the difference.

Attracting Men to the Church

Hispanic men must be attracted to the church. Unless we win them, we will not win the family. Every effort must be made, therefore, to build the church around the family—of which the man is the head. Here I want to give a few suggestions on how to attract men to the church. It goes without saying that we should *never* use the world to attract men into the church. Lowering our godly standards to accomplish this end is self-defeating.

The pastor, a man's man. The pastor is a natural leader, the most visible example, and the main source of influence over men. It helps when he possesses a natural physique which makes him stand tall, above or equal to his brethren. Lacking that, he can still be a man's man in a number of other ways. He must be "one who manages his own household well, keeping his children under control with all dignity" (1 Timothy 3:4). A henpecked minister or one whose children run him is not going to attract other men. A minister's wife should never usurp his authority or contradict him in public. She would do very well to let him run the church. Even when he teaches a class where his wife is present, she should not volunteer for any discussion or question. If men know he runs his home, they will be attracted to his ministry.

The pastor must not be a woman's man. That is, he must not cater to the women of the church. He should not call them or talk to them without their husband's knowledge and permission. He should be known as a man's man. But won't he appear to be cold and aloof to the women? Yes, but it is better to be acceptable to the men than to the women. No man wants to expose his wife or daughter to a man whom he can't trust. Too many pastors turn the men off by talking to and touching the women of the church. Learn this lesson well, and men will be drawn to your ministry. Talk to the men instead. Seek them out. Spend time with them alone. Let them know you want to be with them, not their wives. The men respect that kind of man.

Develop and display manly characteristics. Young men with boyish faces should grow a mustache. It adds years to your life. Let your hair turn gray. It helps. For years I had difficulty attracting older men to our fellowship. One year I let my beard grow, and it came out black and white. It put ten years on me, but it also attracted a number of older men to come to hear me. I don't have the beard now, but the men are still with us.

Have a firm handshake. It always impresses the men, as does a firm *abrazo* ("embrace"). Women should not be embraced unless they initiate it, and even then it ought to be a polite response only. But the man should know you have feelings for him. Weak, sickly handshakes are a sure turn-off. Along with this should go a good smile and a strong word of welcome, appreciation, or acknowledgment.

A final word on appearance. A pastor should dress like a man. He should never wear effeminate clothing, nor should he dress like a little boy. I wore white pants with white shoes to work one day. An older man advised me against it, and I quickly learned the lesson. A pastor in America should dress formally like the local banker. Informally, he should dress like his father or grandfather. Cutoffs, sneakers, T-shirts have their place, but not on the church grounds or on visitation. Most of my people have not seen me without a shirt and tie. Some have not seen me without a coat. Don't be legalistic, but remember to be a man.

Make men visible. Another way to attract men to the church is by making men visible in the church. Any man visiting your church should know by appearance that your church is a man's church. This means ushers who are older men. Teenage boys should not be allowed to usher at the main church services. They can be used in the evening services or with a healthy mixture of older men. Men should lead the program, give announcements, lead in songs and prayer, take up the offering, and do anything else that takes place in front of the people. Obviously special numbers, choirs, and special events can be exceptions to this rule.

Men should teach the adult classes. Men want to be discipled by a man. The Sunday school class is a discipleship class and will be avoided by most men if the class is taught by a woman. Exceptions to all these principles abound, but I am speaking of the norm. Have men conduct the adult classes even if you have a gifted woman. A woman should not be drafted to teach an adult class just because the men in the class won't teach. Better to wait for the Lord's provision than to violate a basic principle (see 1 Corinthians 14:34–35; 1 Timothy 2:11–15). You will also have greater success at building a good youth group and junior high and high school program if you get good men to lead them.

Men attract men. If the pastor makes a special effort to place real godly men before the public, he will do much to attract other men to this message. A man wants to know God has something to say to him. He wants to feel he won't lose his masculinity or leadership if he becomes a Christian. It is easy for pastors to allow themselves to place women in the forefront because Hispanic women are more vocal, more daring, and more outwardly religious than the men. The minister or leader must resist this temptation. He must work to make the men highly visible.

Preach to men. A sure way to attract men to the church and to the gospel is to preach to them. Make the sermon masculine. Let me add that I believe there is no biblical justification for a woman to be a pastor. Moreover, it violates the social order of the Hispanic culture. I can't agree with the Pentecostal woman who said to me, "Well, if the men won't do the job, then the women must do it."

Pastor, preach to the men. By that I mean, prepare your messages with the man in mind. Preach to his needs, to his sins, to his problems. Take care not to preach to the men because their wives spoke to you during the week. Don't allow the women to use you as a tool to get to their husbands. Talk to them straight from the heart. They appreciate a man who deals with them as a man. Don't beat around the bush. Be open with them. Just remember to make sure you are doing what you want them to do. Men abhor hypocrites.

Preach to the women on behalf of the men. In many of our churches, the men are made to be the real sinners, and the women the saints. We judge a Christian by the wrong criteria. The men drink, smoke, cuss, lust, and don't come to church activities, so preachers have a field day with them. A man doesn't mind being rebuked as long as his wife has equal time from the preacher. The preacher must preach to the women about their sins too, like gossip, insubordination, covetousness, slander, sloth, vanity, hypocrisy, short tempers, and vengeance. A pastor preaches to a man when he helps the man straighten out his wife and kids.

Organize around men. The church should be organized around the men of the church. The elders and deacons should be men, as we have just mentioned. If deaconesses are permitted, they should serve the deacons. The main ruling body of the church should be made up of men, in accordance with the qualifications of 1 Timothy 3:1–13 and

Titus 1:5–9. The men in the community should be informed of who makes up the leadership of the church. Sometimes it may mean revising an existing church constitution which has women making decisions for the men of the church.

Subcommittees and class committees should be chaired by men. The women like it when men take these responsibilities, and the men rise to the challenge when it is expected of them. One of our classes postponed elections until a man could be found to run for president of the class. The women absolutely refused to take that position.

Emphasis both in the church bulletin and from the pulpit should be directed to those programs that appeal to men. Rummage sales, bake sales, women's auxiliary meetings, and clothing distribution programs are just not appealing to the men. These activities need the pastor's support, but they don't need to be played up from the pulpit. Soul winning, teacher training, seminars, building funds, missions, and other functions are attractive to men. Remember, the average male is thinking of ways to solve the world's problems, not about the amount of flour in the cake mix.

I don't at all want to minimize the work of women in the church. They have kept many a church going when the men have abdicated. But the church is not where it should be because the pastors have not built their churches around the men. If we can get a man saved, committed to the local church, and active in the ministry, we have all he has—his wife, his kids, his talents, his funds, and his energy. If you just get his wife, you get her and the little she can give with her husband's permission. So get the man and keep him!

HISPANIC WOMEN

Our women have been the subject of many love songs where lovers speak of their *chiquita* in Monterey or their *conchita* in Acapulco. I shall not endeavor to explain all the virtues of Hispanic women or expose their weaknesses.

The Role of Women in Society

Men may be the head of Hispanic culture, but women are the heart and hub. They influence our culture in more ways than we want to credit them. It's because of this influence that Christians and church leaders must pay such close attention to them and their ways.

The heart of the home. Machismo may give the directions, but *mamacita* ("mom") gives the emotion. In reality, the woman provides the warmth, the care, the personality of the home. A man may influence by his power, the woman does it by her presence. The cold, emotionless attitude of a father is counterbalanced by the warm, approachable qualities of the mother. This distinction is so pronounced that the practice of the veneration of Mary gains its support more from this cultural pattern than from the Bible. The unapproachable God is moved by an approachable mother to answer a son's request. Hispanics can all too well identify with this.

The obvious contrasts can lead to many domestic problems. Children divide their allegiances. The mother may win the children to her side and mount an offensive against the father. The children, especially the boys, may grow up to be cruel and cold in deference to dad. Usually a gulf develops between mom and dad, sometimes leading to divorce and separation.

Yet one cannot overlook the benefits of this trait. The family has a warm fireplace where the children feel loved and accepted and where the husband can find consolation in his time of need. Laughter usually permeates the house. Everyone feels good about going home. Think of what this can do to a good church!

The treasury of spiritual truth. Hispanic religion has traditionally been matriarchal. For one thing, the mother raises the children and provides their first religious instruction; then the nuns (*madrecitas,* or "little mothers") take over as the church's instructors. For another thing, the religion caters to the mind set of women.

Hence, Hispanic women are by tradition the natural treasury of spiritual truth. For this reason, they feel a deep burden to impart their newfound faith to their family upon conversion to Christ. They're generally successful with the children but find an obstinate heart with their men. Actually, the man has been obstinate all the time to the reality of God's laws, but the "new religion" is a challenge to his leadership. He must resist, at least for the sake of his ego. If the woman remains patient, does not preach to him, and lives a consistent (not necessarily perfect) Christian life, he will eventually begin to sympathize with her new faith.

A woman will be more receptive to the Word, more desirous of becoming involved, and more sympathetic to spiritual things than a man. Wisdom must be used to bring her into the faith without offending her husband. Even in evangelical Christianity she will continue to have a key role in giving spiritual direction and stability to her home.

The idol of all. Women become the idol of our society. She becomes embodied in *Mamacita Querida*, ("the beloved Mother"). Our moms can almost do no wrong. They hold some kind of invisible spell over us. In later years, as she grows old, she seems to draw her "little flock" towards her. Her children love her, protect her, defer to her, and, in short, idolize her. A woman grows lovelier as she ages—and more loved. Her warmth repays her in the cold sunset of her life.

The Characteristics of Hispanic Women

Let me list some general characteristics of our women, the ones that set them apart from their Anglo counterparts. They are neither superior nor inferior qualities, just distinct.

1. Submissive. Hispanic women are generally submissive. They give the leadership to the man. Women liberators are frowned upon! The Hispanic woman sees her place as being next to her husband, to obey him, to raise the kids, and to share his life. Even in the worst of marriages, a mother may advise her distraught daughter, *"Es tu esposo. Te debes de quedar con el!"* ("He is your husband. You need to stay with him.") Divorce proceedings are rarely initiated by women except in extreme cases. She wants to serve her man, just like her mom!

Her submissiveness, however, can lead to her abuse. The *macho* man may take advantage of her cooperative spirit, and a wife can easily become a maid to him. She can become a doormat to him and may suffer greatly at the hands of a cruel, compassionless man. One must be careful how the issue of submissive wives is taught to a mixed audience. Actually, it is necessary to temper the whole idea of submission with a true biblical view, not the one ordinarily taught to liberated North American women. I constantly warn them to be *mancitas pero no mencitas* ("meek, but not idiots").

2. Compassionate. Our women are warm and tender, full of mercy and compassion. This also makes them romantic. They have a heart for others which makes them extremely hospitable, and children love them. Their great love for children makes them poor disciplinarians to the point that others may consider their children unruly. They make great children's workers in ministry, but they are less effective with teenagers.

The fact that they are so nice and desirous of making situations agreeable also makes the issue of honesty and fairness difficult. They may not look at a lie as an evil, but rather an effort to make someone feel comfortable. Absolute honesty is elusive for some women, but their intent is not malicious because it stems from a deep desire to please. This can frustrate a preacher. In time the issue is laid bare as sin! But until then it is good to understand the motive.

3. Homekeepers. The Hispanic woman tends to be a homebody. She sees herself in the role of mother and housekeeper, performing her task with calm diligence and absolute delight. She wears her apron with a sense of pride. Even among poorer families, she would rather endure a lower standard of living than abandon her nest for the glamor of more wealth. But cultures are in conflict in America, and some women live deeply frustrated lives because of the tension between careers and keeping the home.

4. *Female-oriented.* The Hispanic woman wants to be around other women. A peculiarity of Anglo women is that they like to be involved in the circles of men, to enter into their discussions and their work. Hispanic women leave the men alone and congregate to discuss more personal or feminine matters. It is common for men to say of a woman who doesn't abide by this rule, *"Alli viene la vieja metichi"* ("Here comes that busybody"). Anglo women need to learn this important principle.

On the positive side, this allows the women to work hard in women-oriented ministries. It also supplies a deep need of women to confide in other women. They feel fulfilled as a result of "women talk." The men also express themselves more when only men are present!

5. *Industrious.* She is a beehive of activity, especially around the house. It is easier to get them involved in church work than it is the man of the house. Work is a challenge performed without too much complaint. Obviously, every culture has its lazy sloths. Ours has its fair share. But it's refreshing for a pastor to know that he is working with a group of women who are not afraid of a little work. Man, put them to work! You'll be glad you did!

6. *Impulsive.* This may be a trait of all women, but Hispanic women seem to jump before a full assessment has been made. Whether in words or deeds, this can become a headache for church leaders. The amazing thing is that since it is so widely done it doesn't cause a whole lot of harm. There is more smoke than fire.

There are other things we can say about our women. They are usually more abreast of what goes on at home, and even at church. They usually handle the money and pay the bills. Being more emotional, they are more expressive. In short, they also have the traits of women the world over.

The Ministries of Women in the Church

Perhaps it would be well at this point for me to assess some of the ministries which women may be involved in without jeopardizing the overall momentum and growth of the church. As fellow heirs of the grace of life, women are obviously entitled to all the privileges of God's children, which also include the exercise of their gifts and abilities. These privileges, however, are also subject to biblical principles and to cultural patterns. One must be wise!

Women as pastors. Although there may be many Hispanic churches with women as pastors, my personal conviction is that God's Word is quite explicit about the position of pastor being reserved for the male gender (see 1 Corinthians 14:34; 1 Timothy 3:1; 2:11–12; Titus 2:4–5). This conviction is not based on a chauvinistic view of life, but on the plain statements of Scripture. However, even if the Scriptures were silent on the issue, it would be culturally unacceptable for a woman to stand and preach to men. The evidence shows that this is truly ineffective in the Hispanic community. Women preachers serve primarily in small churches and not in the mainstream of the Hispanic religious community. This is a useful sociological observation.

The ministry to women. Hispanic women have a wonderful opportunity to minister to other women. They really respond to one another well. Since so little has been done in the area of women's ministries among Hispanics, very few opportunities exist. The chances for ministry are so well-established that I would challenge every pastor or leader to exercise some imagination and a little dare. The result will be fabulous.

A few years ago we tried a new program for women called, "Women of the Word" (WOW for short). The women met on Monday evenings and Thursday mornings for discipleship. The leaders were all women. The results were great. These small groups bonded the women, challenged them, trained leaders, and met a real need in discipleship. The women loved it.

The ministry to children. Perhaps nowhere else do our women excel more than in their ability to get to the hearts of children. Their maternal instincts and experience make them naturals at children's ministries. One word of caution. It will help the boys a great deal if churches place men along with women in the ministry to children. We strive to have husband-wife teams all the way from the nursery to the adult classes. This gets the man involved, but it also shows the boys that ministry is a man's job too. It seems to be working.

The ministry to the church at large. Every church needs a woman's touch. In the effort to gain the man, do not neglect to make ample use of the gifts and talents of your women. Give careful guidance to those women whose husbands are not saved. A little patience on their part may draw him into the gospel net before she outpaces him beyond reach! But nonetheless, women are at the hub of the community, and they need to be at the hub of the church. They will bring warmth and compassion to every group of believers.

8

Preaching to Hispanics

And when they heard that he was addressing them in the Hebrew dialect, they became even more quiet *(Acts 22:2).*

Preaching is my calling, my business, my expertise, and also my delight. I have preached over 150 sermons a year for eleven years, and for over six years I have also taught sermon preparation classes in the East Los Angeles School of Ministry. In this chapter, it will be my aim to share with the reader the specifics of ministering to an Hispanic audience from the pulpit. Much of what I will say has been said in the many homiletical helps in existence today. I myself learned most, if not all, of my preaching techniques from them. Still, ministry to Hispanics requires its own particular focus.

THE PREACHER'S SOURCES

In keeping with the homiletical steps toward sermon construction, it will do us some good to lay down some practical steps in the formation of the particular sermon. Almost every type of sermon follows the same general pattern, but if you have the Hispanic in mind, then it would help to be very selective in the grade and kind of material used in the sermon construction.

Study the Bible. Preaching is always expository, that is, it exposes God's truth. The main source of truth, if not the only one, is the Word of God. Learned preachers should consult the original languages whenever possible. I have found the knowledge of the biblical languages of inestimable value in understanding the Bible and in explaining its truth to the man on the street.

The Bible must be read in its contemporary languages, and this applies also to the Spanish texts. The language of the accepted versions is archaic and difficult for the average Hispanic to understand. I personally prefer an updated translation of the Bible such as the New American Standard Bible or the New International Version because of their accuracy and especially their readability. I don't wish to disparage the King James Bible, but unless the text is readable, it can be a hindrance to understanding the Word. Without getting into any of the textual controversies, let me say that the Word *must* be studied.

I am a firm believer in deep study to preach to simple people. The less education the hearer has the more education is demanded of the preacher. We should not be deceived into minimizing preparation just because we are preaching to simple people. Their problems are complex. The Bible is deep. Connecting the two is quite a challenge. Ministers with less formal training must see their lack as a challenge, not as an excuse for mediocrity. Pity the poor preacher who gazes upon the Hispanic masses as an easy challenge.

Visit the people. After we spend time in God's Word, we must also spend time in God's world. "And the Word dwelt among us" needs to be said of us as well. The preacher must visit with the people. We need to dwell among them. I preach from what I know about people, and what I know I have learned by being among them. The application, the illustrations, the content of what I preach comes from their lives and not from a preacher's homiletical guide.

Once after church, I overheard a woman say to her friend as I passed her, "There goes the man who looks right through you." On many occasions husbands have accused their wives of priming me about them, when in fact I knew nothing about their particular problems. "He seems to be looking right at you," someone said of me. Obviously, the Holy Spirit is making the application of His Word as He promised. But we must give the Holy Spirit something to apply.

In one of my favorite illustrations I compare our fleeing from the light of the gospel with roaches scattering at the turning on of the kitchen light. You can never speak with confidence or authority on subjects with which you do not have firsthand experience. We do not need to experience sin, but we need to be with those who have experienced it or are in the very depths of it. We must be around children to speak on children. We must be around sick people to give the comfort of God to the sick. There is very little we can tell people if we have not descended into their very lives.

People seeking to understand the Hispanic people and their culture *must* spend time with them. This time needs to be spent not in teaching, but in observation. A quick eye and ready ear is of more value in the early stages than a fluid tongue. Young Hispanic men aspiring to be preachers and pastors will find their sermons more powerful when they draw deep from the lives of their people. Visitation is time consuming, but we must be consumed with people. Next to the Bible, our people are the best sources for sermons.

Counsel the needy. Another great source of preaching material is the counseling chamber. We learn to deal with sins and spiritual ailments in public when we treat them effectively in private. We need to make time to counsel people. The average Hispanic cannot afford the luxury of a trained psychiatrist. In addition, the lower classes are inundated with complex problems. The pastor is a natural (and sometimes the only) source of help.

I find the pulse beat of the church in the number of counseling appointments during a given week. I can also tell the kinds of problems the average church member is having. I can therefore plan to preach on this problem as a means of helping others deal with them or avoid them. If we are wise, our counseling sessions can have two benefits. First, we can help an individual. Second, we become aware of a problem that others may be facing too and can plan to preach on it eventually.

Lest this double boon turn into a terrible bust, let me also warn you of some things you ought not do. Never use the counseling session as an example or illustration for a sermon in the church. No one likes becoming the subject of gossip, not even if the person remains anonymous. Never decide to preach on a special problem the same week just because a few people have come to you with that problem. Never take your counseling problems home to your wife and family. They should not know the problems of your people unless the people make it known themselves. Never take their problems personally. Take them to the Lord Jesus. If He can't solve them, then surely you can't either. But by all means, set time aside to counsel the people of your church and community. They will teach you how to preach.

Read the newspapers. A ready source of information about the community and the world is the newspaper. The average Hispanic wants to know about the current events of life. The youth are especially up on the issues and items of interest. A subscription to a Spanish newspaper is a *must* for anyone who preaches in Spanish or is involved in a Spanish-speaking work. Not only will these keep you current, but they will also clue you in on the language of the common people.

Read their writings. A preacher in an Hispanic community must read what others have said about the Hispanic as well as what the Hispanic says about himself. Much work has been done in this area since the social revolution of the sixties. Hispanics are now publishing books, periodicals, and magazines which really highlight their culture. Deep insight into patterns of thinking can be gleaned from a serious reading of this material. Even Hispanics will be amazed at what they didn't know about themselves.

Be observant. Finally, a preacher must be observant. We must constantly be looking at the world around us. A careless, thoughtless preacher will not be able to minister to the needs of his people. But a careful, watchful, thoughtful preacher will know how to preach about the hurts, the disappointments, the despairs, the dangers of his community. Scratch where it itches. Soothe where it hurts. You will do this well if you become observant.

THE PREACHER'S STYLE

"The style is the man," said a famous homiletics instructor. The style I aim to write about is not the kind of style discussed in most homiletical helps. Rather, I want to write about the style of preaching which appeals to the general Hispanic populace. Paul held the attention of the Jews because he spoke in their dialect (see Acts 22:2). That was his style with the Jews. Hispanic preachers and those who preach to Hispanic audiences should adopt the same style. Just the other day a young man came up after one of the services to speak to me about his family. He attends a fine Baptist church but he mentioned that he could not take his family there because they could not relate to the preacher. Instead he wanted to invite them to our church because they could "relate" to the preaching. Actually the Anglo pastor in the Baptist church could do the same if he just modified his style somewhat.

Even Hispanic ministers vary in their effectiveness based on their style. So many of us come from the American seminaries geared to the Anglo church. The homiletical instruction aims to produce preachers for the Anglo world. Hispanics who fall into these classes unknowingly adopt a style which is totally unattractive to the Latin mind. Thus they fail at that which they could do best if they followed their natural instincts instead of trying to imitate Spurgeon or R. A. Torrey. I would like to suggest six distinct aspects of style which are essential in preaching to the Hispanic mind. Let me hasten to add, we are not advocating tickling their ears just to get a crowd (see 2 Timothy 4:3–4). What I am suggesting are the flavorings in the Word and the plate upon which the pure, unadulterated Word is served.

1. Organization. Nature is organized, and so is a man's mind. The simplest creation of God has order and so does the most ignorant hearer. A preacher must be organized too. People don't like to be confused. If the point and progress of the sermon are not immediately clear, all is lost. It is not uncommon to have Hispanics walk out on the preacher. My greatest fears are that I may lose my hearers within the first few minutes of preaching or leave them totally confused at the end of my sermon. Get organized!

The preacher should present a simple truth clearly and then drive it home throughout the sermon. Most people can only do one thing at a time, and Hispanics are known for being one-item people. It is counterproductive to introduce two or more parallel ideas into a sermon or to cram too much into one sermon. Rather, keep the idea simple, the development clear, and the whole sermon well-organized. The outline will be your lifesaver. If it is difficult for you to follow, it will be impossible for the hearer. Even if you think it is good and juicy, consider it carefully. Is it something a person has to read to understand or would simply hearing it be sufficient? In short, be organized, and you will have the hearts and minds of Hispanics.

2. Simplicity. "Speak in the language of the common man" was George Whitefield's motto. J. Vernon McGee said,

"Put the cookies on the lower shelf so the children can reach them." Hispanics are for the most part very simple people. Most in North America are not highly educated. This is not to demean them but only to state a truth. How else can we adequately minister to them?

You should speak your sermon in the plainest manner and choose your words carefully. We should not have to consult a thesaurus to find a more difficult or scholarly word. Stick to the simplest term. We had a Yale law graduate come to teach one of our primary Sunday school classes. Right in the middle of the lesson the director stopped him saying, "Wait a minute, who do you think you're talking to? This isn't the Yale alumni association. These are children. Speak to them." These are not the graduates of your finest universities. Speak to them in their language.

Strive to be understood, not to be admired. I have been accused of being too simple, but I would rather be understood than be impressive. When people say to me, "That was a good speech" (newcomers don't know it is called a sermon), I just respond by asking, "Did you understand what I said?" My aim is to preach so that even the most ignorant will understand. An Anglo preacher says he preaches to the top level of his congregation. It might be good for him, but when I visited his church there were no Hispanics in it. In fact, some left our church, went to his, then came back saying, "He loses me in his preaching." If you want to preach to the top level, stay out of the Hispanic church. You see, there is no top level there yet. When there is, then we'll call on you.

3. *Energy.* Spurgeon said there were three essential qualities to a good sermon: "Fire! Fire! Fire!" Dr. John MacArthur said, "Set the pulpit aflame and folks will come to watch it burn." Hispanics deplore dull speech. Think of Fidel Castro haranguing the United States and you get the gist. It's the spirit, the excitement, the fight in the soul. That's what captures the imagination.

The natural excitement of the Hispanic personality is a contributing factor. A typical Hispanic speaks with his soul, not just with his mouth. Hands wave in the air, feet move back and forth, the eyes are aflame and penetrating, and there's an urgency in the tone of voice. This is the way he speaks about everyday life. Can we imagine him accepting the truths of God with any less energy?

Anglo ministers in Hispanic communities can learn to speak with such energy. They need to leave the soft sermons and quiet reflections to more sophisticated orators in white, urban America. When you step into the *barrio* pulpit, make sure you have something to shout about. An Anglo brother who spoke in one of the Hispanic churches received a mild rebuke when the hearers told him he was "dead."

My preaching is energetic. In fact, I've broken a few pulpits in my lifetime. I've jumped on the pews and even on the organ. I've run down the aisle and pointed my finger at people. I once preached a sermon in San Diego where I never raised my voice or beat the pulpit or walked around, and my Anglo brothers thought I was too energetic, too convicting. If only they knew how reserved I had been. That indicates the difference between cultures.

Of course energetic preaching needs substance. If we have nothing to say, no matter how loud we shout or how much furniture we break, the sermon is a waste. We shouldn't be like the windbag tent preacher with no substance, of whom the Indian said, "Bah! A lot of wind, a lot of thunder, but no rain."

4. *Compassion.* Hispanics cry easily. They are a heart people. Faced with the cruel realities of life and accustomed to them, they think with their hearts, not just with their heads. Sermons cannot be just logical; they must be warm and logical. Straight, theologically orthodox preaching without a touch of life is like eating a taco without chili sauce. It falls flat.

Preachers must shed some tears, appear human, even

laugh with their people. At times, we have ourselves in stitches in our services. We laugh at ourselves in the light of the gospel.

We find the Bible is too full of emotion to turn into a cold museum of sacred history. God cares, answers prayers, saves, heals, and even works wonders. Why do we need to turn our churches into seminary classrooms? "Preach with a moist eye," says Jack Hyles. Don't be afraid to be human in front of your people.

5. Illustrations. Preach in parables that reveal rather than hide truth. Jesus used stories, parables, similes, metaphors, and anecdotes to illustrate divine truth. He was the master story teller. He did so because He was addressing the common people. Jesus spoke to the poor, the illiterate, the irreligious, the scum of humanity. Dare we address the same crowd today in a different way? Hispanics are a simple people and like truths plainly stated and well-illustrated.

It is a firm conviction of mine that every scriptural statement needs to be illustrated from everyday life. We should state the truth, give scriptural proof or justification, and then illustrate it from common life. The technique is much too common for me to amplify. Every homiletical help stresses its importance in preaching. Yet, it is amazing how often preachers minimize the need to illustrate their proposition. A dear friend of mine is considered by many to be quite knowledgeable in the Word, and yet he is a boring preacher. Why? Because he refuses to illustrate his points. A sermon is like a good building, well lit. The darker the understanding, the more light we need to bring the truth to bear on the soul.

6. Pointedness. "You need to tell it to us straight, Alex! This beating around the bush won't do. You know how we are. If we can get out of it, we will." A co-worker who addressed me with those words taught me how to preach to Hispanics. Preach specifically, not in generalities. Don't just preach on stealing, make it pointed. "Don't go into the K-

Mart, change the tags on items, and then justify your actions by saying, 'Everyone does it.' You are stealing, and you are a thief!" That's pointed preaching.

Don't just say, "Husbands love your wives." Make the point personal. "If you love your wife you are going to show her you love her by telling her you love her. Now, sir, have you said these words to your wife today? Yesterday? You better start today." That is pointed preaching.

Preacher, take aim and hit something. Don't just "preach the Word" and have the Holy Spirit do His work. Give Him something to work with! Hispanics think in specific terms, not generalities. If you preach pointedly, you may not be popular, but you will effect a change in their lives.

SOME HELPFUL HINTS

Every preacher is unique and develops his own style. He preaches himself ultimately. He rams himself down the barrel of the cannon and fires himself at the people. In closing this chapter, I'd like to add a few more helpful hints.

1. Preach to hurts. If you help someone, they will be back and probably not alone. We should strive to preach to comfort the afflicted, to heal the broken, and to relieve the downtrodden. All theology makes man a better person and a happier one at that. We should never divorce our theology from the daily lives of our people. If our theology does not heal, then it is not biblical. If our sermon does not heal some hurt, then we are worthless physicians doing no good. Think of all the hurts our people have, then preach to heal them. You will never exhaust your material for preaching.

2. Use heart language. When Paul changed from Greek to Hebrew, the audience paid close attention. Why? Because the Jews spoke in Greek, but thought in Hebrew. Hebrew was their heart language. Hispanics also have a heart language. You can discover the heart language in their homes or in their unguarded moments. Whenever I want to get inside the heart, I resort to heart language. Whenever I want to regain a lost audience, I resort to heart language. There is the language of books and another language of life. Be wise in your selection.

3. *The more personal you make it, the better.* Our preaching should be personal. Last Wednesday a class from a local university came to observe our church as a model of inner city ministries. After the service, one of the students said, "Your preaching is very personal. It's as if you know everyone in the audience." I didn't tell him that I almost did know everyone present. I try to preach to individuals, not just an audience. Let them know you are aware of them personally, and they will respond in like manner.

4. *Avoid preachiness.* Avoid the whole idea of giving a sermon. We have not been called to entertain or to perform for people, but to declare the whole counsel of God. We should have something to say—and say it with energy—to achieve our end of bringing people to God. If we are mere pulpiteers and not prophets, we adulterate the high calling of God. Hispanics are not accustomed to sermons. They want to hear what God has to say.

5. *Strive for eloquence.* Words convey truth. We must learn the use of words. In fact, we should become a master at words so we may choose the correct word for the proper thought. Hispanics admire eloquence. They will gladly listen to you if you know how to communicate. Pulpit ignorance is not only disgraceful, but harmful to the cause as well. One word of caution though. Don't let your learning be a hindrance to the cause.

6. *Be patient.* Think of Moses struggling forty years with the nation of Israel. How they must have tried his patience.

It takes a long time to build a church, even longer to build a good church. We must possess the patience of Job if we are to make headway in this ministry. Hispanics do not have a long heritage of gospel living. Those who labor now are building a foundation. If you persevere, you will see the rewards of your labor.

It's been eleven years since I first accepted the challenge to build an Hispanic work. Only now am I beginning to see the results of years of building. What if I'd quit after three or four years of service? It takes a long time, but the rewards are unspeakable. My advice is this: if God calls you to an Hispanic work, prepare for a long, difficult, exciting, and ultimately, very rewarding ministry.

9

Hispanic Morality

But you are a chosen race, a royal priesthood, a holy nation, a people for God's own possession, that you may proclaim the excellencies of Him who has called you out of darkness into His marvelous light *(1 Peter 2:9).*

There are significant differences between Hispanics and Anglos in their social practices and morality codes. For example, Hispanic women are more chaste in dress and conduct, less given to the vices of smoking and intoxicants, less rebellious and domineering, and less materialistic. They are more "motherly" than American women and less apt to get abortions or file for divorce.

The Hispanic community does have its problems, however. Certain sins have become part of the culture and are accepted as the community norm. It is the responsibility of the Christian church neither to ignore these practices nor to condone them as "cultural distinctives."

These issues must be addressed because they are like a cancer slowly destroying Hispanic society. *"Por eso estamos como estamos"* is a saying we use among ourselves when we honestly face these issues. The phrase means, "That's why we are in this condition."

When the gospel enters a society, it has a transforming effect on the individual, the family, and even the culture. What others may consider merely "cultural traits," the Bible sees as sin. Formerly acceptable practices become unacceptable. For example, when the gospel comes to New Guinea, cannibalism among the tribes becomes unacceptable.

Hispanic culture also has its accepted practices that the Bible rejects as unacceptable. I would like to lay before you seven of our greatest heartaches, sins which are deeply rooted in the culture.

Drunkenness. Rare is the home which has not been blighted by alcohol. Drink—strong drink—permeates the Hispanic culture. The Catholic priest drinks wine to appease the conscience of the masses, and the man in the pew drinks *tequila,* a very strong drink, to appease the anxieties of life. Both end up as alcoholics. As many priests have drinking problems as do the people they serve. Hispanics drink at baptisms, weddings, funerals, parties, and for no apparent reason at all. Sometimes they start a *fiesta* just to have an occasion to drink. Other times, they begin a work project not to complete the job but for the sake of drinking. Others may think of us as a fun-loving people, but we are a people too often controlled and devastated by alcohol.

One tires of addressing a poor mother whose husband consumes his meager wages on drink; who instead of buying the bare necessities of life for his starving and naked family, deposits his hard-earned cash at the corner *cantina.* He comes home to wreak havoc on his family, beating his wife, spewing out vile words and vomit simultaneously, breaking what few possessions they have, then retiring into a drunkard's sleep until the next day. You want to know the real cause for our poverty? It's drunkenness. To our drinking society, it may seem like too simplistic an explanation. But when we honestly face the issue, drunkenness lies at the root of many of our social evils.

Drink, like any drug, gives a temporary euphoria mistaken as happiness, but in the end it bites like a viper. Death is sure and slow. In the end it makes its victim many times more miserable than the poverty he was trying to escape, or the homelessness he was trying to forget. The drunkard is a miserable wreck, a despised fool, the laughingstock of the community, and usually the victim of a bitter, lonely death.

The pressure to drink is very strong. The males have no place to turn. Drink is *the* pastime of the Hispanic male. The Hispanic male who does not drink is either sick, cowardly, or a religious freak. In short, if one does not drink he does not measure up to the *macho* ideal. The young look upon the old man who can't drink because of ulcers or cirrhosis as a has-been or a weakling. Even an older man who converts to Christ and preaches against drinking is looked upon as a man who couldn't hold his liquor. Thus, he's less than a man! If a man doesn't drink, what does he do? Where does he go? With whom does he associate?

Christian churches and Christian ministers cannot ignore these realities. They must provide meaningful alternatives to this lifestyle. First, the church must make clear the evil of drunkenness. The Bible states quite clearly that drunkenness is sin, a soul-damning sin (see 1 Corinthians 6:10; Galatians 5:21). No excuse, no apology, no compromise, no sociological or medical explanations need be offered in defense of drunkenness. It is sin. The people are so conditioned to accept drinking as a pleasure given by God that it takes a long time to turn this mentality around. We must carefully teach what the Bible says about drinking, so a new generation of believers can be raised who do not accept the dominant Hispanic view.

The church also needs to counter the social pressure to drink by holding up an alternative image of what makes a man. In the Christian community, a man is not measured by how well he can "hold his liquor," but how he measures up to a true definition of masculine character. Reread the chapter on men to underscore the importance of true masculinity. Our men do not really know what a man truly is. They can only parrot what their fathers and grandfathers did before them. The pulpit must be a constant reminder to our men of what a man must be.

To counter the social pressure, the church must also

provide meaningful relationships and activities for our men. The church is often permeated with women's circles, studies, and get-togethers, but the men are left idle with nothing to do and no one to do it with. A serious men's program must be organized which effectively ministers to a man's needs. The program should make it possible for a man to make new friends, to get involved in meaningful activities, to learn principles so he can properly guide his home, and to simply enjoy being the man God intended him to be. Almost any program which provides these four things will help keep men from caving in to the social pressure to drink.

Finally, the church must prepare itself to minister to the devastating and long-lasting effects of drinking. It must be able to provide funds for destitute families, shelter for the wife and children when they flee the rampages of the drunken father, counseling for families of alcoholics, detoxification centers and halfway homes for men in desperate need, and warmth and understanding for families with no immediate relief in sight. The problem won't go away overnight. For some it will be a lifelong nightmare.

Sexual immorality. Another plague on our people is sexual immorality. The whole culture turns a blind eye to the husband who has a mistress on the side. Somehow men feel more *macho* if they are able to bring more children into their lives by means other than through a monogamous relationship. So they perpetuate this immoral practice. The music, literature, movies, and even religion of the culture put their stamp of approval on this lifestyle. Ironically, the husband can have his escapades, but the wife must be loyal.

This double standard is destructive to our culture. We have become desensitized to it. We scarcely blink at its deleterious effect on ourselves, our spouses, our children. Immorality degrades the woman: the mistress becomes a common whore, and the wife becomes the household maid who is expected to serve all the needs of her unfaithful man, from sex to raising his kids. All this without a word of protest.

Whatever respect and affection existed is swept away by this mode of infidelity.

The children are the most affected by this moral confusion. They must eat the dust of poverty. When the father takes a mistress, he starts bringing less money home. Whatever scraps the family originally had, they must now share with others, and no explanation is even given to them. They feel betrayed by a man they call their father who now spends less time with them and whose heart is not with them. Even his words sound hollow and meaningless. They feel betrayed by their mother who quietly accepts this fate for both them and herself. They see her shrivel into a cowardly, hopeless maid. They cannot understand why she does not stand up for her dignity. But worse, they will grow up to perpetuate that which they loathe in their hearts and which they are powerless to escape. Why? Because culture dictates that this is the way Hispanic families live.

The whole cultural pattern needs changing. Society is heavily affected by this perversion of sacred trust in the matrimonial relationship. Alongside the poverty and family brokenness, Hispanics experience emotional trauma: damaged self-esteem, a feeling of inadequacy, a detachment from commitment in marriage, and a certain feeling of lostness. There is ample evidence of this among the children in Hispanic families.

Sexual immorality must be exposed as sin. We must not commit the twin errors of being mute about the matter by not preaching against it, or of condoning it by allowing such men and women to consider themselves good Christians. Sexual immorality is a shameful (1 Corinthians 5:1), dishonoring, (Hebrews 13:5), treacherous (Malachi 3:14), and damnable sin (1 Corinthians 6:9–10). We must muster all the weapons of spiritual warfare and lay siege to this vice until it is fully exposed for what it really is, a detestable violation of the marriage union.

Next, we must show women how to demand respect and maintain respect in the Hispanic society. All too often the doctrine of the submissive role of women has proved to be pernicious. True, women are to be submissive to their husbands, but we all know that submission ends where human dignity is threatened. We can be doorkeepers, but not doormats. We may wash the feet of our fellowman, but to kiss his toes? In Spanish we have a saying for our women, *"Sea mansa pero no mensa!"* It is a play on words: "Be meek, but not stupidly weak."

We must teach women to expect respect from their husbands and to demand it from them. They must be taught that dignity is more important than security and that real love is better than any cheap counterfeit called romance. Our women must realize that they have gospel rights, and that among these are the right to be treated like women, the right to divorce an unfaithful husband (see Matthew 19:1–10), the right for the church to honor a lawful separation (1 Corinthians 7:1ff.), the right to vindication by the church against an unfaithful husband (1 Corinthians 5:1–13), and the right to expect help in time of need (Acts 6:1; James 1:27). A woman who is the victim of this cowardly act is in many ways worse off than a widow.

The church must then learn to deal with the children in these relationships. Special care must be given to demonstrate real love to them. Boys often become cold and bitter toward their fathers. They distrust men and have a difficult time showing their feelings. Boys also lack the proper male image and so lose the opportunity to learn responsibility and other characteristics of a proper manhood. Girls, on the other hand, become like mama, even to the point of adopting her lack of discernment or ability to stand up for her dignity. Craving for a father's love, they often fall prey to the advances of a man much like their father, and the cycle begins once again.

Children must be given proper role models. We dare not parade men or women who have been guilty of these things and present them as "good Christians." Leadership from our churches must be taken from among the proven pure and not rom the promising prominent. Give them examples they can mitate. Show them from Scripture the true scriptural pattern or the family. Be severe with the guilty and merciful to the penitent.

Abuse. A third unexposed sin is abuse. Hispanics have a ong history of violence. The *conquistador* was a man of violence in search of conquest and treasure. The Aztecs and others were people of bloodshed, with little regard for human life. Hispanics respect strength and sometimes elevate it to dangerous levels. To them, the sword is mightier than the pen.

Violence is a way of life. The rich abuse the poor. The strong abuse the weak. The men abuse the women. Parents abuse their children.

Here the church must take a stand. Hispanics look upon suffering as someone else's problem. Yet, we cannot stand idle as we see a people "distressed and downcast like sheep without a shepherd" (Matthew 9:36).

Our silence permits a two-caste system—the rich and the poor, the honored and the despised, the intellectual and the peon. The trouble is that we permit this injustice in the name of evangelism. We tolerate bigotry and selfish ambition in the name of ministering to the "upper class" and "lower class." These distinctions may exist in the Hispanic world, but they shouldn't exist among Christians. We dare not sacrifice the poor on the golden altar of upper class evangelism. We are not after the "most influential element of society." We seek to bring the elect, the lost from all sectors of society, into one body, the body of Christ.

Abuse can take the form of physical abuse. Hispanics exalt the sports of boxing, bullfighting, cockfighting, and gang warfare. Abuse can also be seen in the home where the husband makes it part of his routine to beat his wife weekly. Somehow, it is real *macho* for a man to bring his wife into submission by any means, even by beating her. I have had wives hesitate for years to tell me their husbands were periodically beating them because they were afraid of the wrath of these men.

The church must speak against this harmful *machismo* trait. A real man wins his wife into submission by his love and character. Only a weakling and a coward needs to beat his weaker vessel into submission. The church needs to deal harshly with wife beaters, child molesters, and the like. It must provide the stamina behind the one in need of help.

Deception. Many cultures are prone to exaggerate. Hispanics practice a form of deception arising from a desire to please and be hospitable. An Hispanic is so willing to please that he may even lie openly to keep your friendship. The culture has learned to live with this kind of deception, and you see it everywhere. The church lies to the poor peasant to keep him faithful and to aid his faith. The government lies to the people. The merchant lies to the buyer, the farmer to his workers, and even a friend to a friend.

Deception and lies take on certain cultural patterns. In the marketplace the best deal goes to the biggest liar. The bribe is so commonplace in Latin America as to be ruinous to a novice. Rarely is political graft dealt punishment of any kind. It is almost expected that people go into politics to make off with a certain percentage of the public treasury.

In the church, the same patterns show up. People lie because they think that God can neither perceive their deception nor provide for their needs. They lie out of fear. The church must foster a new outlook on God's ability to see both their deceptions and their needs.

Deception must be addressed clearly and divorced from culture. We can be honest and still be nice. We can tell the truth without offense, and when necessary, we must also tell the truth and offend. Offending someone because of the truth is better than deceitful kisses.

The minister himself must live by the principle of truth, then he must preach truth and its merits, and finally he must expect truth from his congregation. Sometimes this appears brazen and rude to the Hispanic, but we must learn the true definition of love. Real love is truthful.

Irresponsibility. North Americans have stereotyped the Hispanics around them as lazy, irresponsible, and habitually late to everything. And to an unfortunate degree, Hispanics have to bear responsibility for this, not for personal but rather for cultural reasons. The contrast between Hispanic and North American culture is quite evident when literally millions of Hispanics invade the American mainstream of life. Thus there are immigrants rubbing shoulders with middle-class America. What usually happens is, an undisciplined, lower-class Hispanic has to compete or coexist in a highly structured, disciplined community.

Life south of the Rio Grande is slower, less demanding, and often less developed. There is no real need to hurry to meet schedules. We have all day to do it since nothing else is on the agenda. It's like eating an ice cream cone: why hurry if there is nothing else to eat afterward? Why not savor it, instead? Remember, the poor, with no expectations of advancement, don't worry much about time and discipline.

Once in America, however, the Hispanic is faced with a serious dilemma: change or suffer the consequences. Adapt to American economic realities or be doomed to inevitable poverty. The church must help the Hispanic make the proper adjustments. It must teach its people to be on time, to set goals, to plan, to do more than one thing at a time, to keep pace with the vast and rapid changes of our complex American society—all of this, without losing the excellent qualities of Hispanic culture.

The problem is that Hispanics may balk at these changes. They see nothing wrong with starting services late or showing up late. At one ladies luncheon, a group of ladies showed up two hours late and still expected to be served! Somehow we need to impress upon our people that such conduct is socially unacceptable in American society.

Other areas of responsibility needing attention are child

rearing, money management, school attendance, job performance, civic involvement, and ministry in their local church. We need to hammer away on these areas until our people get the message that irresponsibility, for whatever reason, is not proper Christian stewardship. It's a long, hard process, but not an impossible task. There is no reason why we cannot lift ourselves and our people from the mire of irresponsibility.

Disloyalty. It must be the mark of the poor and oppressed that they trust no one. The greatest loyalty of Hispanics is to the family, and then to God as they see Him. But outside of that, loyalty comes hard.

I've worked among both Anglo and Hispanic churches and have been able to see the vast differences in this aspect of loyalty. For instance, Anglo ministers develop a certain comradeship and loyalty to each other. They not only seek each other out, they also place a great deal of confidence in each other. Hispanic ministers have a different air about them. They don't trust each other, they rarely work as a team, and they peck each other to death in their drive to be the chief *caudillo* preacher. Obviously, this is not going to help the cause of Christ in the *barrio.*

All our weaknesses converge on this point to produce a suspicious leader, unable and unwilling to work with anyone else. Such pride and independence is sin. We must examine our hearts carefully to rid ourselves of such contamination. We must pluck the plumes of pride off our silly heads and put on the garment of humility worn by our Lord Jesus Christ. Loyalty to Christ and His church should be our chief end. Apart from that we are nothing.

The best way to teach loyalty is by practicing loyalty. We Hispanics have grown up in an atmosphere of fear, hurt, and betrayal, but we can overcome disloyalty by fixing our eyes on the Almighty God who richly supplies all things for our enjoyment, who raises and lowers men at His will, and who promises to exalt the humble and abase the proud (see James 4:6, 10). Loyalty must be preached, practiced, and paraded before God's people until we glory in men like Peter instead of mimicking the deeds of Judas Iscariot, who stabbed his master in the back for a few silver coins.

Idolatry. Hispanics are an idolatrous people. From the twin civilizations—Indian and European—they inherited a tendency to worship materialistic images. Hispanics have temples, altars, statues, pictures, candles, and holy objects. All our culture is steeped in idolatry.

The Catholic church has been the major influence in promoting idolatry. It has syncretistically adopted pagan Indian worship practices and mixed into it a bankrupt form of Christianity brought over from the Old World. Though some argue that the church has images merely to remind worshipers of the realities behind them, church leaders too often condone the practice of praying to others besides God, of kneeling before the statues, of holding to "sacred superstitions" about them. The church has never openly condemned this practice and thereby violates the commandment of God (see Exodus 20:4; Matthew 15:3).

We must openly confront this practice and show how it violates the commandments of God. And we need to show a God who is able to answer prayer, is concerned with the affairs of man, and has provided access to His throne through His Son, the Lord Jesus Christ. Idolatry thrives among the ignorant and misguided. They need the clear teaching of God's Word, for it is the light that reveals the childishness of idol worship and the seriousness of trying to appease a jealous God with trivial excuses for our idolatry. May God help us to lay the issue of idolatry clearly before the people in our churches.

I have singled out these various sins because they have become so entrenched in our culture. But there are many other sins which we can deal with as Christians working among Hispanics. We need to expose our own sins, confess them, and live upright because a holy Christian is a happy Christian.

POSITIVE ASPECTS OF HISPANIC MORALITY

Not all is bad in our culture, but I have tried to deal honestly with aspects of the culture that Hispanic leaders often gloss over. At the same time, Hispanics are not the most wicked people in the world. They have some great virtues to teach North Americans and the rest of the world. In pure Hispanic settings where the culture has not been contaminated by North American influence, we can find some endearing qualities.

La persona. Hispanics value the worth of the person, *la persona.* Anglo-Americans are task-oriented. Hispanics are people-oriented. Winning your friendship is more important than gaining your business. Listening or hearing about your family is more important than the business at hand. Since modern society is constantly resisting the pressure of an impersonal society, it is refreshing to find a people who value you on the basis of who you are as a person and not on what you have. Christianity gives worth to the person; materialism robs him of value and dignity.

It's my practice to walk out into the audience after every service to mingle with the people. The other day an Anglo visitor said to me, "It's refreshing to see the leadership spending time with the people!" I knew what he meant. Too many ministers pull a disappearing act after service. They do not want the people close to them. Exactly the opposite is true of Hispanics. The person is more important than the program. Actually, in the end, all you really have and need that is worthwhile is people. Without people, one is hopelessly alone.

Hospitality. Akin to the virtue of *la persona* is the Hispanic emphasis on *hospitalidad,* hospitality. Aloof, impersonal, fast-paced Anglo-Americans have a rough time understanding this quality. At first it is seen as an imposition or a great waste of time, but there is much good in this quality.

Hospitalidad shows up in the desire to get to know you by spending much time with you, usually around a meal. Anglos rarely visit anyone unannounced, even if they are family. I've had some really close friends visit who won't even sit down for a cup of coffee. An Anglo visiting an Hispanic home, if he is welcomed inside, will usually be offered something to eat or drink. It's good if he doesn't refuse. This is not just a token gesture; it's real hospitality. One gains more by receiving, even if it's just a quick drink. Poor people have little else to offer except their hospitality. If you reject this, you reject the only thing they really have.

By the same token, Hispanics don't feel they need an invitation to visit you. They may show up at your door unannounced and may throw your afternoon plans into chaos. They expect good treatment too! They've come to visit you, to show you they care, and that they like your company.

Perhaps this is what is meant by "hospitable" (1 Timothy 3:2) and "Let love of the brethren continue. Do not neglect to show hospitality . . ." (Hebrews 13:1–2).

How can such interruptions be a virtue? When we consider the loneliness experienced by so many North Americans in our impersonal society, it's refreshing to find people who still have time to simply sit down and talk to you. To me, it's refreshing. I just can't stand those "butterfly visits."

La verguenza. Another very positive trait possessed by Hispanics, especially Hispanic women, is known as *la verguenza,* ("a sense of shame!"). Hispanics are shocked by the apparent absence of shame in Anglo Christians. Things we take for granted and without much remorse here in America, Hispanics both here and elsewhere see with a different attitude. By Hispanic standards, Anglo Christian women are immodest in dress and behavior. It's not uncommon for Anglo Christian women to go to church in shorts, wear bikinis in mixed bathing, and dress in tight pants or short skirts. During our trips to Mexico, the Anglo leaders had to tell the teenaged girls who were going down to convert the "infidel Mexicans" not to wear shorts or miniskirts, so as not to offend the Mexican women. This seemed ironic to me. But it shows the different standards.

The lady's behavior with her boyfriend or suitor is viewed as a thing of honor and decency. Chaperones are still in fashion. Curfews are in order. Certain activities are prohibited. I've had unsaved Hispanic fathers call to complain about indecent "American" behavior of men toward their daughters. I've had to do a whole lot of explaining since their daughters were dating supposedly "Christian" men! The church today could use a good lesson on decency and "shame!"

El dolor. Hispanics know a few things about suffering too! They are not afraid of *el dolor,* ("the pain"). People accustomed to not having, to suffering, to hurting, to enduring pain without complaining are best able to show God's power over difficult circumstances. They often become "mute Christians under the smarting rod!" Hispanics are not afraid of "dirty work" or "humble circumstances." They also make fearless fighters and courageous athletes. In church life, they learn how to "do without" with a thankful spirit. Men have learned especially not to be "cry babies," but "to grin and bear it."

The future of our Hispanic churches will lie in the hands of these men who are not afraid to suffer, who will not mind the pain, ridicule, and deprivation of the Christian ministry. It is not a place for "soft, sissy men." God will raise up men acquainted with sorrow, suffering, and grief. Upon these the gospel mantle will fall. They and women like them will build the churches of tomorrow. May God make us all equal to the task.

10

Worship and Music

Let the word of Christ richly dwell within you, with all wisdom teaching and admonishing one another with psalms and hymns and spiritual songs, singing with thankfulness in your hearts to God (*Colossians 3:16*).

Worship is extremely important to Hispanics. For centuries under Catholicism, Hispanics were placed under a form of religion which emphasized the centrality of worship. The rituals of the mass, the rosary, and holy days of obligation necessitated a congregating of the faithful. Churches were holy places where God lived, and to meet God people had to go to church. In short, worship took place in the church building.

The sudden change to evangelical Christianity can be traumatic for some new converts. Christian churches are bare structures. Notably absent are the statues, pictures, candles, and stained-glass windows. A pulpit and communion table replace the altar. The pews have no kneelers, and the preacher faces the people. The rituals are replaced by a corporate relationship to one another and to the spiritual presence of God. The emphasis is now on the Word of God and not on the sacrifice of the mass. Excitement replaces the quietness, fellowship the solitude, and joy the permeating gloom.

Theology governs our worship. Catholics worship one way because of their theology, whereas the theology of evangelical Christians necessitates a different form of corporate worship. The priesthood of the believer eliminates the hierarchy. The finished work of Christ eliminates the rituals of sacramentalism. The security of the believer eliminates the gloom of uncertainty. The primacy of the Word eliminates the ecclesiastical ordinances. The fullness of the Spirit brings in a corporate celebration of victory and encouragement, eliminating the solitary struggle for acceptance before a wrathful God. In seeking to form patterns for worship, these theological truths must be prominent in our minds.

I do not prescribe a new order of worship, for then I would be placing the church under another yoke of ritualism. Each body of believers develops its own unique style of worship. I would, however, like to accentuate some essential characteristics which seem to be present in Hispanic churches. These are mainly cultural, part of the Hispanic personality.

Worship should be informal. A peculiarity of Hispanic worship services is that they are loose. They don't usually stick to a tight schedule or a prescribed order of worship. When I left the Anglo church in suburbia and visited an Hispanic church I marveled that they sang for thirty minutes. The service started at 7:00 and singing continued until 7:30. After a few other testimonies, the preaching began at 8:00 and lasted until 9:00. It was nothing like the neat, one-hour evening service I was so accustomed to in the Anglo church. No Hispanic seems to mind this arrangement.

The service needs a little time to warm up, a little time to cool down. You will be disappointed or will develop high blood pressure if you expect to start a service on time with everyone there. I was a speaker recently at a large conference for Hispanics. Leaving home in plenty of time, I got caught in the notorious traffic jams of the Los Angeles freeways. As the traffic crawled, anxiety gripped my heart. I knew I'd be at least ten or fifteen minutes late. I'd forgotten where I was going. I should have known we'd start forty minutes late anyway. These are the kinds of things to expect.

Here's the point: keep the service loose. Start on time, but wait for people to get there before you enter into the more serious aspects of worship. Don't let the small incidental portions bother you. They don't seem to bother the congregation as a whole.

Worship should be warm. Hispanics are a warm, loving people in general. They expect warmth and love to be part of the corporate worship experience. That's why some Hispanics don't enjoy going to Anglo worship services. They say the services are too cold and formal. They need a measure of warmth. How is this achieved?

Laughter and expression should be encouraged. One church has a song with a chorus: *"Dame la mano"* ("Give me your hand"). During the singing of this part, the entire congregation shakes hands with as many hands as possible during the length of the chorus. The songleader and songs should be warm. The preacher should be a warm, enthusiastic person. The offering time should be a happy time.

Some people equate quietness and somberness with worship. To Hispanics, a warm, energetic service is just as worshipful, if not more so! For some people, it is the *only* time when they actually feel loved and experience the love of God. Don't aim for a quiet worship service. Aim for a warm worship service.

Worship should be festive. Hispanics make their worship a form of celebration. It is not unusual for people to bring their own instruments—women their tambourines, and men their guitars. Others clap their hands while the whole church sings. The service sounds like a huge pep rally, yet it's a true expression of worship. The level of intensity varies from church to church. The real success of the Pentecostal church has been to release the congregation to celebrate the Lord in the service. Other denominations working among Hispanics can learn a valuable lesson there. It's not theology but worship that makes the difference.

We always needs to guard against excesses, obviously, and to take precautions that the church service is adequately balanced with the other elements mentioned in Acts 2:42. But we do need to be open to other cultural patterns of expression.

Worship should be spontaneous. Hispanic worship services thrive on spontaneity. By this I mean the element of letting people express themselves during the worship service. In some churches, while the leader prays, the entire church erupts in audible spontaneous praying. They all pray and seem to know when it's time to stop. The audible praying slowly stops and silence reigns until the next portion of worship is introduced.

Spontaneity can also be manifested in loud responses to the preacher's message with such expressions as "Amen!" "Hallelujah!" or *"Asi, es"* ("That's the way it is"). Our audiences also clap for what pleases them. Care should be taken not to stifle a spontaneous response to worship based on traditions or preconceived, nonbiblical opinions on worship.

Worship should be responsive. In some churches, about the only response one gets from a congregation is the responsive reading or the exit at the end of the benediction. Hispanics, however, like to respond audibly and visibly in worship. They do it most obviously in the warm, loud singing. If you notice the crowds that respond at evangelistic rallies, you have no doubt been amazed at their size. Much of it stems back to audience response. It is possible to have the whole church come down the aisle in response to an invitation after a soul-stirring message. In some ways, this is peculiar to Hispanics. It's a manifestation of their need to respond physically.

A preacher must be careful not to abuse this need or to harden the heart by foolish and inappropriate invitations to a public response. A wise leader must use discernment in calling for these public demonstrations of God's touch upon the soul.

Let me paint for you a picture of a typical worship service.

As you arrive at the church a few minutes before the scheduled time of service, you find some worshipers gathered. Some are outside talking and sharing spiritual truths. Others are inside conversing, excited about what is to take place. Hardly anyone is sitting quietly in meditation. You are struck by the kaleidoscope of apparel. No particular style of dress stands out, but they are all clean and modest. Ostentatious apparel is noticeably absent.

The service does not begin on time. No one seems to mind. In fact, the church is not even half full. The crowds continue to trickle in for the next thirty minutes, and keep doing so until the last few minutes of the service. Mothers bring their children in with them, and you wonder how they manage to get anything out of the service. Somehow you sense they do. You also marvel that even the little ones know what is going on. A little seven-year-old girl claps her hands and sings along with all the rest.

The song service seems endless. There is no real order to the songs or the service. The songleader is enthusiastic and seems to follow the mood of the service. Yet at just the right moment, he turns the service over to the preacher. You've been standing for the last ten minutes. Now he leads in prayer. In this church, they all bow quietly and say "Amen" at the close of the prayer. The pastor then greets the congregation and encourages them to greet each other. The response is enthusiastic and jubilant. These people seem to know one another. After a while they are seated and the preacher gives a few announcements.

The offering is taken. You notice their faithfulness, and notice for the first time the percentage of young people in the audience. Not only do the young people like to serve, but the church makes ample use of them. The offering is simple. There's no long, drawn-out appeal for money. The people seem to sense that this part of the service is a sacred moment.

After the offering plate passes, the people do not remain silent. A buzz begins to rise as the plates make their way toward the last pew.

More music follows. Another prayer. Perhaps there is a testimony by a brother or sister. Someone sings a special number. It's obvious there is more heart than talent, but the people don't seem to mind, and everyone is attentive. The choir sings an anthem or a joyful song. It's happy and pleasant, but again you can't hear much harmony, and the sopranos are simply graduated altos. Again, the people love it. Either no one has an ear for music, or no one really cares how they sound as long as the love of God is there. You sense the latter is the truth.

Finally the preaching begins. The preacher opens his Bible and announces his text, and from all over the church you hear the rustle of pages as the people race to find the passage. The people stand to read, they pray, then they are seated. The preacher begins to unfold the message. His style is energetic, passionate, and direct. He screams. He points. He pounds the pulpit. He whispers. Occasionally he walks up and down the platform. The message, however, is thoroughly biblical. He interweaves stories and anecdotes. He has the people laughing one moment and stunned the next. Finally he draws the sermon to a conclusion. He prays for a long time and then makes an appeal. It seems you're the only one left in the pew.

The preacher sends the folks back to their seats and after a song the congregation is dismissed. As you make your way to your car and out of the parking lot, you notice that many are lingering both inside and outside the church. Forty minutes after the benediction, the deacons will be escorting the last people out of the church so they can turn off the lights and close the door. Even then some will stay long after you are safe at home. You get the impression that even more is accomplished after the service than during it. Then you realize that this fellowship too is part of the worship. People have met God, and God has met their needs.

MUSIC IN THE CHURCH

A whole volume should be devoted to a study of music in the Hispanic church. Here we mainly wish to touch on a few matters of importance to the preacher and church leader. Music is a vital part of the Christian life and of church worship (see 1 Corinthians 14:26; Ephesians 5:18–20; Colossians 3:16). A good music program is as essential to church life as a good sermon.

Adopt an Hispanic hymnology. Music is culture expressing itself. What has truly gripped the heart will come out in music. The Hispanic community has done exactly that through its music. It expresses its philosophy, its joys and sorrows, and even its theology in music. Latin America has no standard type of music. Every nation seems to have its own peculiar style, and even within a nation you will find divergent styles of music. Hence, a universal Christian hymnology has not yet been established for the Hispanic churches of Latin America.

The situation north of the Rio Grande is different. Here the Spanish-speaking churches are often linked with North American denominations, many of which have made the effort to translate traditional English hymns into Spanish and publish Spanish hymnals. Some of these contain original Latin American compositions with a distinct flavor, but on the whole they reflect the music of North America.

The Hispanics in English-speaking ethnic churches use the contemporary English hymnals. They have no other option, and actually do quite well. What affects them also affects the Anglo churches. These churches have the advantage of a bilingual music ministry. Our church sings from a traditional English hymnal, but we add a few of our Spanish songs. The result is exceedingly uplifting.

Guitar versus organ. In many Anglo churches the organ and piano are sacred instruments. A certain church in San

Diego even taught that the guitar was sinful. Another in the East regards all music in the church as sinful, except for that produced by piano and organ. We need to set the record straight for the Hispanic church.

We must realize that the guitar is *the* musical instrument of Latin America, and hence of all Hispanics. The basic purpose of the guitar is to give the beat and the pitch, thereafter depending on the skill of the one playing it. The guitar can be used to entertain, but it is not a sinful instrument. Just as the piano and organ can be used to play ungodly songs, so too the guitar has a place in the worldly affairs of the Hispanic. But keep in mind, it is *the* musical instrument of Latin America.

The guitar must be allowed to be part of the worship services of Hispanic churches. In many cases, if not most, it will be easier to find a good guitar player than a competent pianist. Organists are extremely rare. I do not recommend electric or bass guitars as suitable instruments.

The *mariachis*, the Hispanic quartet or ensemble, sing the ballads of the common people. This format can be used to express the Word of God. In some instances, this type of music brings back memories from the world and so should be used and developed with discretion. We will see the day when the gospel will be placed in ballad form for the benefit of the common people. It may well be the Christian *mariachi* who will teach the Hispanic the gospel songs.

Caution about choirs. We have tried for ten years to get a church choir going, and we still haven't been successful. As I write this chapter, our pianist has resigned because the music is too difficult, leaving our choir totally despondent. In fact, I can't think of any Hispanic church that has a choir worth shouting about. Some have choirs, but they are mostly well-meaning folks who have joined together to sing for others with one of them waving his hand in front. I have yet to see an Hispanic choir put on a decent version of Handel's *Messiah*. There is something missing in our people.

The missing factors are various. First, the Hispanic church does not have a long history of singing. Most of the churches sing without any previous knowledge of music theory or without any idea of harmony. In fact, harmony is not essential to the worship of God or even for soulful expression. But harmony *is* important to a church choir, for music must be pleasant to the ears at least. God may look at the heart, but men must listen to the tones. Trained voices are hard to find. There is also a noticeable lack of soprano and bass ranges among Hispanics. Maybe it's the mixture of Indian blood. Nevertheless, good choirs need good sopranos and basses.

My advice is simply this: Don't worry too much if you can't have a good church choir. It is more important that our people learn to sing to the Lord than to people. If we can inscribe the hymns in their hearts, what does it matter if we cannot cut a record with our choir? Don't misunderstand me. Work at a choir. We need good music, good musicians, good composers, good choirs, and good choir directors. We also need to develop a good hymnology. These will come in time if we work on it, but let us be careful not to sacrifice the true value of music and its place in the Hispanic church.

Zeal in songleading. The average Hispanic thinks the Anglo service is dead or boring, because of the style of music and preaching. We have discussed the latter in the chapter on preaching. Latin-American music is lively. Even when the theme is dead, the music is still lively. The stately, solemn hymns of German churches do not stir our souls. The revival songs of Moody and Sanky, along with the evangelistic choruses, are pretty well down our alley.

The Hispanic church should have a zealous songleader, one who has *chile* in his blood. Hand-clapping, soul-stirring music is what the people prefer. A reserved, melancholy songleader will kill almost any worship service. But get a man up there with the joy of the Lord, with fire in his blood, and a good selection of gospel hymns or songs, and the church is in for a good time of edification. There are times at which I am afraid to preach for fear of cooling the inspiration produced by the song service. The opposite also happens. A bad song service dampens my spirit in preaching.

The songleader is to assist the pastor in the service, not act on his own. The songleader works *for* the pastor, not with the pastor. He must be willing at a moment's notice to change a hymn, cancel a special number, sing another stanza, or anything else the pastor might deem essential to the song service. He must be submissive to the leadership of his pastor and must be so with a good spirit.

Keep singing in perspective. Songs are to be sung. The problem with the dying church is it doesn't sing enough. A church service where special music outnumbers the congregational songs is one where death and spiritual decay are knocking at the door. People need to sing. They need to sing because troubled hearts find comfort in songs, happy hearts express their joy in songs, and theology is ingrained in the emotions through songs. People who do not sing are spiritually sick. I can usually tell if one of the members is backsliding because he will not sing. A canary will not sing when sick; neither will a sin-laden Christian.

A typical song service in our churches involves a few selections made by the songleaders, a couple of special numbers, and some selections from the congregation. The songleader usually begins the service with a song that has a lively tempo and gives the service a sense of expectation. The hymn before the message is a slow, prayerful one, setting the mood for the Word of God. I prefer a soloist before I speak. This helps to quiet the heart. We find if you let the congregation select the hymns, they usually select the hymns they like to sing, in which case you will naturally have a good song service. Our song service also alternates between guitar and piano throughout the service. In short, the song service should be a time for God's people to express themselves, not a time-filler.

11

Conclusion

"Do you not say, 'There are yet four months, and then comes the harvest?' Behold, I say to you, lift up your eyes, and look on the fields, that they are white for harvest" (John 4:35).

When opportunity knocks, the wise person opens the door. We too would be wise if we looked at the Evangelicals' opportunities to reach an entire segment of our population for Christ. In our fifteen years of ministry in Los Angeles, we have witnessed the growth of the Hispanic evangelical community from a tiny shrub to an impressive tree. I have been amazed at the Holy Spirit's work among us and have been absolutely ecstatic over the result of a few years of labor among such a rich harvest of souls.

It is only fitting to close this book by offering you a challenge not to overlook this great opportunity, not to despise the "minority" group, not to neglect to participate in reaping where others have sown and to sow where others can reap. Every Evangelical in America can have a part in this work. Let me challenge preacher and layman alike to consider the potential of the Hispanic churches.

YOUR CHURCH CAN GROW

It has been said that the average size of the Anglo church in America is one hundred. The average size of the Hispanic church is less than fifty. Traditionally, the Hispanic church in America has been characterized as a small mission station or storefront church of around fifty people or less, with a lay preacher, struggling to survive. This scenario hasn't inspired too many people to be identified with the work. Nor has it motivated our Hispanic men to consider the challenge of the ministry. Rather, the whole ministry was an embarrassment to the work of God, and it lacked credibility among the mainstream of the Hispanic community.

But things have changed. The fact is that Hispanic churches are growing, and growing substantially. In our local ministerium of Hispanic evangelical pastors, a few of the churches easily number in the hundreds. Montecito Heights Christian Church, under the leadership of Pastor Ezekiel Salazar, had 900 in attendance recently. Primera Iglesia Biblical Fundamental, pastored by José Fernandez, numbers over 500. The Bell Baptist Church of Bell-Cudahy is over 400 strong. The Bilingual Baptist Church of Pico Rivera under José de Leon has over 500 attending. Montebello Baptist Church has between 200 and 300 people. First Fundamental Bible Church of La Puente has 250. Several churches have passed the 1,000 mark, including Templo Calvario of Santa Ana, California, under Pastor Daniel de Leon, which has around 2,500, and First Baptist Church of Hammond, Indiana, which averages 1,600 a Sunday.

It is increasingly evident that the Hispanic church is no longer a storefront ministry, nor is it just a small mission station. The church is growing and can continue to grow. Pastors of small Hispanic ministries need to catch the vision of church growth, and need to begin to help their congregations get the vision. Getting out of a rut or state of depression is difficult for any minister, but it is especially difficult for our Hispanic ministers. May God help us to enlarge our borders. Look up at the harvest. Look at your brother who pastors a growing church down the street. *Hermano, sí se puede!* ("Brother, it can be done!") The same phenomenon can take place under your ministry.

YOUR CHURCH CAN BE INDEPENDENT

Another source of great encouragement for anyone laboring in the Hispanic mission field is the great thought that your church can be independent. By that, I do not mean the ecclesiastical or denominational structure known as "independent churches." I mean the independence from the Anglo mother church, or as we often see it, "the smother church." The Hispanic church has come of age and is rejoicing in a newfound independence.

Hispanic churches are now financially independent. They are no longer missions subsidized by someone else. They support their own pastor, build their own buildings, and foster a missions program. For too long the Hispanic church has been a part of a spiritual welfare state, which produced an anemic clergy and an equally immature and pathetic congregation. But having lifted themselves up by their bootstraps, many churches can now boast of a new independence and a new spiritual vitality.

The emergence of the middle class and the inroads of the gospel into this group have yielded many benefits. Gifted, talented, and experienced Hispanics have been won to Christ, and they have taken the mantle of the ministry. Unlike the middle-class counterparts in Latin America, they have not despised or forsaken the poorer Hispanics in America. Wealth is not a status symbol, but an instrument of ministry.

Templo Calvario recently raised over $2 million to purchase a new facility. Victory Outreach of Los Angeles bought a school for $1.75 million. Our own operational budget is $37 thousand a month, and our offerings exceed our expenses by $100 thousand a year! The point is this: these are Hispanic churches, not wealthy, middle-class, Anglo ministries.

Independence applies also to organizational structure as well as to autonomous dealings. More and more, we see our churches desiring to run their own ministries and succeeding at it. Over and over we see churches pastored by

Hispanics rather than Anglo missionaries. For years some Hispanics (and Anglos) have said, "We cannot run the churches without the oversight of the Anglo churches." Well, we have seen it happen again and again.

Our Hispanic leaders need to know and believe that they can manage without constant oversight and control from the Anglo ministry. If we change our palms-up, beggarly attitude to a palms-down, on-the-plow attitude, we shall see the church really take off. If we but learn to plant our own seed, water our own plants, and reap our own crops, then we shall enjoy the abundant fruit of our own labor. Many Anglo leaders are realizing that a doling ministry produces a dull church. Hence, they are urging the Hispanic churches to become independent as soon as possible.

Independence gives the preacher and his church a certain sense of dignity and self-respect. It also makes us proud of a distinct heritage while not losing sight of our own position as Americans and fellow workers with all other saints. I would challenge our preachers to cast off their fear and indolence. Lead your church to full financial and organizational independence. Consider that you are just as capable and your people just as competent to manage, sustain, and extend their own ministries. What are you afraid of? *Hermano, sí se puede!* If you look at others who have done it, you will be motivated to do the same.

YOUR CHURCH CAN REPRODUCE

For too long, the Hispanic community has been the mission field of the Anglo church. Now something new is happening. The Hispanic church is finding out that it can reproduce—it can be instrumental in propagating the gospel and establishing new works. The Hispanic church is now looking at its community as its own responsibility.

The church used to have (some unfortunately still do) a myopic view of itself, caring for its own needs and remaining self-centered and pathetically unconcerned with the *paiza-nos* ("fellow countrymen"). The church has awakened! In 1985 more than twenty-five hundred delegates came together in Garden Grove, California, to the Congress on Evangelism. The sole purpose of this Hispanic conference was to stimulate the church to reach the Hispanics in North America. This was indeed impressive. Under the leadership of evangelist Alberto Motessi, the *congreso* (as it was called) proved to be a great testimony to an awakening concern for Hispanics by Hispanics in North America. The theme was "*Si no nosotros, quien? Si no ahora, cuando?* ("If not us, who? If not now, when?")

Our church alone has been instrumental in the establishment of six distinct churches. One church in Mexicali has established ten others. If we but catch a vision for reproduction, we can see God using us to spread His church all across America. Almost any pastor can have a part in extending his boundaries if he is willing to eliminate or deal with the fears which hinder most. As I share this concept of church extension with some, I notice a hesitation based on fears. We must deal with those fears.

Our Lord said, "Unless a grain of wheat falls into the earth and dies, it remains by itself alone; but if it dies, it bears much fruit" (John 12:24), and "It is more blessed to give than to receive" (Acts 20:35). With these two promises, Hispanic pastors can approach church extension with excitement instead of fear and hesitation.

Church extension does cost. It costs money, manpower, and membership. There is also a psychological setback in decreased attendance or absence of key people. Then comes the burden of building new friendships and leadership. But then we must ultimately ask ourselves, isn't this what church growth and church extension is all about?

We recently split our congregation to begin a new work in an adjacent suburb about ten miles away. Initially we experienced all the aforementioned costs, and yet just five months later we have almost recouped the losses we experienced with the split. As a pastor and leader, I must always keep in mind certain issues so that God will continue using us in church extension.

For instance, God honors His word. Investments in God's church are always just that: investments. Neither the pastor nor the church loses. Also, we need to believe in our own abilities. If God used us to build His church to a certain size, then what is to prevent Him from doing it again, and again, and again? Furthermore, with such a ready harvest field, there will always be plenty of work and plenty of fruit. Think also of your experience. If it took you ten years to build a congregation of six hundred people, it will take you much less time the second time around because of your acquired experience and knowledge. In short, take a chance in church planting. You have nothing to lose and everything to gain.

Sometimes I just like to sit and think about the works God has allowed our church to establish and the pastors which have gone out from our church. It thrills my heart. The other day I preached at one of those churches, and I was absolutely amazed by the excitement of God's people there. Here was a church packed with Hispanic believers, and I had a small part in it. It made all the toil worth it.

YOUR CHURCH CAN BE HOLISTIC

Someone said, "Give a man a fish and you feed him for a day. Teach a man to fish and you feed him for a lifetime." Our ministry among Hispanics can be either of these. If we do the former, we will suffer burnout. If we do the latter, we will retire in bliss and pass the torch to a new generation.

Our people have problems, lots of problems. The church must learn to deal with these problems. In days gone by the churches would fall apart because they couldn't deal with these problems. They had converts, but they couldn't heal their hurts and couldn't teach themselves to minister to one another.

I spoke once to a graduate of a prestigious evangelical seminary about ministry in the Hispanic community. He said, "Alex, I feel that my gifts and education would not be fully appreciated in the Hispanic community." In other words, he was too educated and too talented for our people. I responded, "You'll need all of your talents and education, and a whole lot more to minister effectively to such a people." The Hispanic community needs the best preachers the church can produce.

By the same token, anyone wishing to minister to the whole church must so prepare himself. Too many self-styled evangelists and homespun preachers cannot lead the people beyond John 3:16. Anyone too lazy or too haughty to prepare adequately for this ministry deserves the shipwreck and the life he is doomed to receive. If you are called to serve, you are also called to prepare!

We are seeing good men filling pulpits in our churches— men who are ministering to the spiritual, emotional, and physical needs of our people. The gospel not only saves, it also lifts. We are seeing not only souls regenerated, but whole lives reclaimed. Families are being stabilized, children are being trained for life. Hispanic Christians are being channeled into the mainstream of American thought and life. In our own church we have lawyers, dentists, vice-principals, teachers, CPA's, and a host of other professionals. They, in turn, are concentrating their skills on the other people in the church. For instance, our CPA's offer free financial planning to our needy families, which in turn helps them "learn to fish for themselves."

Hispanic counselors run a drug and alcohol abuse clinic in the church. Others, ex-felons and concerned believers alike, help the boys in juvenile detention centers. Our ladies conduct seminars on mothering, being a wife, and simply being the women God wants them to be. We sponsor baseball teams for young and old alike. These are just a few of the many programs we have that attempt to minister to the total person. You can do the same thing in your church.

YOUR CHURCH CAN INTEGRATE
INTO AMERICAN LIFE

Some Anglo-Americans see the Hispanic community as a minority subculture. True, some Hispanics do fit into that category, but there is an ever-growing segment which does not see itself as a subculture. They view themselves as an integral part of America; first Americans, then Hispanics! Some Hispanics have shied away from gathering together as Hispanics because of the fear of being labeled or the fear that, once identified as Hispanics, they will not be assimilated into the American mainstream.

The church is coming of age. Both Hispanics and Anglos view the church as an integral part of American life. English-speaking Hispanic churches are now a permanent fixture. Hispanic men are even being accepted into Anglo pulpits or where Anglos make up the majority of the congregation. This is most encouraging. Even the Spanish-speaking congregations see a need to prepare for a transition into English in the future and to give their young people instruction in English. Wisdom has triumphed over blind nationalism.

We have passed through a crisis of cultural identity and have come out a better society. We see a new America, an America with a plurality of cultures yet distinctly American. If any minority is to really survive, it must learn to assimilate American life, which entails a casting off and a putting on. Hispanics have come to understand this process. The church is part of the process.

Young Hispanics need not fear the *barrio* or the *barrio* church. Rather, they must see themselves as the instruments of change and the bridge between the two worlds. They must see the *barrio* as a challenge, not as a prison. They must see it as a child ready to be born and ought not abort it. "White flight" set back the influence of the gospel in the *barrio*. "Brown frown" may bury the *barrio* in hell. Young Hispanics, lift up your eyes and see what challenges, what opportunities, what a rich harvest awaits you. Don't flee from the Hispanic church. Run to it. It needs you and has long been ready for you. You Hispanics in Bible schools and seminaries, I would especially address this admonition to you!

I offer my personal experience as a challenge for your Hispanic ministry. Through adversity and success, the Lord has shown us what a great joy it is to serve in an Hispanic church in an Hispanic community. I wish the same to all who labor among Hispanics. The purpose of this book is to help you obtain that joy. I trust it will serve its purpose by God's grace.

Select Bibliography

Allen, Roland. *Missionary Methods: St. Paul's or Ours?* Grand Rapids: Wm. B. Eerdmans, 1966.

Arn, Win. *The Pastor's Church Growth Handbook.* Pasadena: Institute for American Church Growth, 1979.

Bennett, Charles. *Tinder in Tabasco.* Grand Rapids: Wm. B. Eerdmans, 1968.

Dussel, Enrique. *A History of the Church in Latin America.* Grand Rapids: Wm. B. Eerdmans, 1981.

Foster, George M. *Tzintzuntzan.* Boston: Little, Brown, 1967.

Harvey, H. *La Iglesia: Su Forma de Gobierno y Sus Ordenanzas.* El Paso: Editorial Mundo Hispano, 1980.

Harrell, Guillermo. *Proyectos Para Mejores Templos.* El Paso: Casa Bautista de Publicaciones, 1970.

Hodges, Melvin. *On the Mission Field.* Chicago: Moody Press, 1953.

Holland, Clifton. *The Religious Dimension in Hispanic Los Angeles.* Pasadena: William Carey Library, 1974.

Horowitz, Irving Louis. *Masses in Latin America.* New York: Oxford University Press, 1970.

Kammerdiener, Donald. *El Crecimiento de la Iglesia.* El Paso: Casa Bautista de Publicaciones, 1975.

Miranda, Juan Carlos. *Manual de Iglecrecimiento.* Miami: Editorial Vida, 1985.

McGavran, Donald. *Church Growth in Mexico.* Grand Rapids: Wm. B. Eerdmans, 1963.

_____ *Understanding Church Growth.* Grand Rapids: Wm. B. Eerdmans, 1970.

Reina, Ruben. *The Law of the Saints.* New York: Bobbs-Merrill, 1966.

Tippett, R. R. *God, Man and Church Growth.* Grand Rapids: Wm. B. Eerdmans, 1973.

Wagner, C. Peter. *Su Iglesia Puede Crecer.* Barcelona: Libros Clie, 1980.

WITHDRAWN

N
F.
J
N.
O

WITHDRAWN